Taking Risks from the Unconscious

Taking Risks from the Unconscious

A Psychoanalysis as Experienced from
Both Sides of the Couch

Donald M. Marcus

And Hope

JASON ARONSON
Lanham • Boulder • New York • Toronto • Plymouth, UK

Published in the United States of America
by Jason Aronson
An imprint of Rowman & Littlefield Publishers, Inc.

A wholly owned subsidiary of
The Rowman & Littlefield Publishing Group, Inc.
4501 Forbes Boulevard, Suite 200, Lanham, Maryland 20706
www.rowmanlittlefield.com

Estover Road
Plymouth PL6 7PY
United Kingdom

British Library Cataloguing in Publication Information Available

Library of Congress Cataloging-in-Publication Data

Marcus, Donald M., 1924-
  Taking risks from the unconscious : a psychoanalysis as experienced from both sides of
the couch / Donald M. Marcus.
     p. ; cm.
  Includes bibliographical references and index.
  ISBN-13: 978-0-7657-0483-2 (pbk. : alk. paper)
  ISBN-10: 0-7657-0483-8 (pbk. : alk. paper)
  1. Psychoanalysis—Personal narratives. I. Title.
  [DNLM: 1. Psychoanalysis—Personal Narratives. 2. Case Reports—Personal
Narratives. 3. Physician-Patient Relations—Personal Narratives. 4. Unconscious
(Psychology)—Personal Narratives. WM 460 M3227t 2007]

  RC504.M254 2007
  616.89'17—dc22   2007016636

Printed in the United States of America

♾™ The paper used in this publication meets the minimum requirements of
American National Standard for Information Sciences—Permanence of Paper
for Printed Library Materials, ANSI/NISO Z39.48-1992.

From Donald Marcus:

To all those who have taught me, and especially to my patients—past, present, and future—and to my wife and daughters, who have encouraged me to be present and responsive from my heart, rather than from some perfect persona I thought I was supposed to be.

From Hope:

To my husband, my sweetest dream, who taught me sacrificial love and acceptance of what the weather brings.

And to Don: Thank you for not interpreting! Thank you for being true.

~

Contents

~

Introduction

When two personalities make emotional contact at an unconscious level as occurs in good psychoanalysis, emotional turbulence occurs (Bion 1987). An important function of the analyst is to contain this emotional turbulence in the consulting room so that it can be experienced, named, and thought about. This emotional turbulence may be so frightening that either or both parties may wish to end it by taking action or by breaking the contact. The case presented in this book is one in which both parties took the risks required to maintain contact, and it was these risks which seemed to be responsible for the exceptionally good outcome.

The material in this book is an attempt to convey the essence of this experience as seen from the point of view of both participants. Curiously, in searching the Psychoanalytic Electronic Publishing (PEP) archives, I could find no reports of psychoanalyses with comments by both patient and analyst. I am aware of four books where the patient's views are presented, but this book is different in that it is a joint effort. While I, as analyst, had intended to write about this person's analysis because many of my interventions were unorthodox and the results were especially gratifying for both of us, the impetus to write it jointly came from my ex-patient (also an analyst) about a year after the formal termination of the analysis. Prior to this time, we had had only one postanalytic contact, an exchange of letters that occurred shortly before the Christmas holiday season, four months posttermination. This exchange of letters captures the spirit of the whole analysis.

In a letter dated December 19, 1999, Hope wrote:

I wish you a most wonderful holiday season from my heart. I hear of you occasionally, and it comforts me to know that our lives continue intertwined.

I remain thrilled with our splendid finish! I am telling everyone that analysis really can come to a perfectly artistic close, full circle. I am so pleased and thankful. I even had a dream recently that I was meeting with Dr. K [her previous analyst] to explain without bitterness what I thought had gone wrong between us, and to hear from him. As I was leaving, I took his face in my hands and said, "Now take care of yourself and be original!" I feel quite free now to reconcile with him and think I shall not pass up such a wonderful opportunity. Thank you! Be well.

I wrote back six days later:

Thank you for your beautiful letter. As happened so often during our time together, it went from my brain to my heart, where it touched me and had a healing effect. I had been wondering recently how your emotional heart was, and if our ending was truly as good as we both thought it was. Somehow, you managed to give me just what I was looking for.

My scientific brain does not believe this, but my heart sometimes thinks you were sent to me as a wonderful gift to encourage me to dare to be the best I could be. As with Dr. K in your dream, you helped me be original.

I am deeply grateful.

I was intrigued by the idea of writing together, but I wished to wait until at least five years had passed so that we could be reasonably certain that the results were lasting, and to allow our unconscious minds to think about it. As it happened, three and a half years posttermination I was asked to present some work at a conference, and the paper we were planning to write together seemed to be ideal for that occasion. Although our original idea was to write the paper jointly, when Hope's time became limited because of her husband's illness, we decided that I would write the paper and Hope would add her history and comments whenever appropriate. Hope was to have the right of final approval of the text. She made very few changes. She corrected my factual errors and used a pseudonym to protect her privacy as well as that of others referred to in the clinical material.

The initial version was almost one hundred pages long and had to be shortened for the presentation. In this book, I have restored most of what was cut and have added three clinical vignettes that I had forgotten at the time of the first writing. In addition, I have added a postscript containing excerpts from our e-mails that allow the reader access to Hope's current status, now some three years after the initial writing. It is worth noting that we have had no face-to-face meeting since the analytic termination. Our communication has consisted of only about a half-dozen phone calls and many e-mails.

The plan of this book is simple. We will begin with a chapter on the ethics of an analyst writing jointly with a former patient, following which we include a chapter on our views of the unconscious. Then we will each introduce ourselves and tell how we met and chose each other. Vignettes from my notes will follow. The notes were all written from memory, usually on the day of the session. No attempt has been made to improve retrospectively on the quality of the analytic work as reported in the notes. The falsification, if any, is in the initial writing of the notes. All of the notes are presented in as close to chronological order as possible. Nothing has been omitted insofar as it was in the notes. I have no doubt that some of my poorest work did not find its way into my notes, but enough remains to give the reader an idea of what transpired. Both the patient and I will comment on the notes in an effort to clarify what we each believe was occurring. After this, we will each try to understand what was transformative about this analysis. Finally, there will be the excerpts from our exchange of e-mails.

~

CHAPTER ONE

Ethical Considerations

Whenever an analyst decides to go public with his work, he must weigh the benefits to be gained against the potential harm that might be done to the patient. Beginning with Freud, it has been accepted that progress in the field requires that analysts present their work truthfully so colleagues can evaluate it. The author usually made minor changes to disguise the identity of the patient, but the essential dynamics were preserved. It was not felt necessary to get the patient's consent; for many years analysts wrote about patients without asking permission, and this was simply accepted as the way it was done. No one paid attention to the potential harmful effect on the patients who might read about themselves. In recent years, as patient's rights have become an important issue, most, but not all, analysts routinely ask for an informed consent. However, as noted by a number of analysts (Aron 2000, Gabbard 2000, Goldberg 1997, Kantrowitz 2006, Stoller 1998, Tuckett 2000), true informed consent may not be possible because of the nature of transference. In carefully reasoned articles, Gabbard (2000) and Kantrowitz (2006) suggest that what is best for each patient must be decided on an individual basis. In her study of patients who were later to become analysts, Kantrowitz found that when patients read about themselves in print, having been asked to give permission was no guarantee that the patient would not later regret having given it. Kantrowitz concluded, "The fact that particular approaches work with some patient-analyst pairs and not with others may have less to do with the issue of writing per se and more to do with either the dynamics of a pair or, at times, a more general problem the particular treating analyst has around boundary issues."

Stoller (1988), in a paper that was before its time, stated: "One would do better ethically and scientifically if throughout the process of writing a publication, we let our patients review our reports of them." In addition, he wrote: "We should not write about our patients without their permission to do so and without their view of the matters about which we write." Stoller advocated a collaboration in which the reader was presented with two points of view and was free to form his own opinion. That is what Hope and I have attempted to do, although we were not acquainted with Stoller's article at the time we wrote. Since the original impetus to write together came from Hope, informed consent would not seem to be an issue. Hope reviewed everything I wrote, correcting factual errors and making changes she felt were needed to protect her privacy. Her opinions are presented throughout. I searched the analytic literature for guidance, but could find only four books (no journal articles) where patient and analyst had written together. Two of the four books concerned the treatment of a psychotic patient.

The first book, Mary Barnes's *Two Accounts of a Journey through Madness* (Barnes and Berke 2002), tells the story of the recovery of a schizophrenic woman through the dedicated, loving therapy of Dr. Berke, who supported her throughout her life. Patient and therapist seemed to work well together in the writing of the book, but I could find no mention of how writing together affected their relationship. As far as I can tell, it was just another aspect of their work together.

Daniel Dorman's book, *Dante's Cure: A Journey out of Madness* (2003), is also about the beautiful, sensitive therapy of a schizophrenic woman. Dorman has written a book where the patient is quoted liberally. On one occasion, they gave a joint paper to a mental health audience. In both of those books no attempt was made to disguise the patient who was the collaborator in the writing.

The third book, by Irvin D. Yalom and "Ginny Elkin" (a pseudonym) (1974), is different in that it tells the story of an aspiring young author with writer's block who is not asked to pay for her once-weekly treatment with money, but rather by writing up her experience of each session soon after it occurred. Yalom also wrote up his view of the sessions, and they did not look at each other's reports until six months had gone by. Yalom chose this way of working because it forced his writer patient to write. It was only after the therapy ended that the dual views of the work were put together by Yalom's wife in the form of a book. Collaborating was an important aspect of the therapy.

Collaborating in writing did not damage the patient-therapist relationship in these three instances, but would that be true if the therapy were psychoanalysis? In a recent book, edited by Schachter (2005), seven analysts were asked to write case reports and to ask the patient to read the report and respond at length. Two of the analysts felt they did not dare jeopardize the analysis by asking the patient, and of the five patients who were asked to write reports, one refused. The book, then, consists of seven case reports by seven different analysts with four patient responses to their particular analyst's report. It is to be noted that there is an extra method of disguise here in that the analyst writer of each case report is not identified except as one of seven, making it almost impossible to link the patient and analyst. Of those patients who read their case reports and responded, collaborating with their analyst was a positive experience. If we assume that the two analysts who chose not to ask their patients to participate may have been correct in their judgment, and also that the patient who was asked to participate and refused may have made a wise decision, it follows that each case must be decided on an individual basis, based on many factors including the two participants, the fit between them, and the degree of success of the analysis. Hope and I were an especially good fit in an analysis that was valuable to both of us. It is understandable that we could write together in a way that would continue to lead to further growth.

In a successful analysis, as the transference/countertransference is analyzed, it is slowly replaced by a real relationship between the two parties, and that relationship is a function of who the parties actually are. My experience as an analyst and supervisor has taught me that in all successful analysis, a powerful loving bond develops, which remains postanalysis. When the patient is also an analyst or an analyst-to-be, as was true of Hope, there is always the question of what the best postanalytic relationship would be. Some analyst patients bid a fond goodbye to the analyst and have no interest in further contact, although there are casual meetings at psychoanalytic society functions. Others collaborate, and still others become friends. There would seem to be no "right" way; each analytic dyad must find its own way.

During this period of writing together, Hope's husband was diagnosed with a slow-growing but ineradicable Stage IV cancer. She has spent increasing amounts of time over four years caring lovingly for his needs—physical, emotional, spiritual, and finally cognitive, as he was overtaken by dementia. I feel honored and deeply touched that she has shared this beautiful experience with me as a friend. There is no way to know if our writing together, and the sharing that has occurred because of her husband's terminal illness, would interfere if Hope wished to return for further analysis, but we both believe that we have not compromised our relationship. As Hope put it:

The patient/analyst boundary remains important after the analysis and always. The analytic experience and relationship/transference is something sacred to be held in trust, even though a broadening of the collegial relationship might very well unfold, as it has with us. I think it has something to do with how important that firm but fluid boundary was in order to be able to do the work safely.

The matter of confidentiality is especially important when the patient is also an analyst. It is usually handled by changing such things as age, gender, and occupation. To do that in this case, however, would create distortions that would be very confusing. For this reason, although Hope has chosen a pseudonym and colleagues are not named, nothing else is disguised. We are aware that those who know Hope well may be able to deduce who she is. On the other hand, we expect that it is the analytic work itself, done almost exclusively in the here-and-now of the session, which will be of most interest to the reader. Perhaps of most concern to professional writers is my choice to respond to Hope from my unconscious, often without processing my response through my conscious mind. This way of working leads to much self-disclosure on my part. Self-disclosure has been written about extensively recently, and I have made my position clear (Marcus 1998). I have concluded that self-disclosure is appropriate if it is in response to the patient in the moment and is not being used to project the analyst's distress into the patient. To some degree, this book is an expansion of the ideas put forward in that paper. It may shock the reader that I have chosen to express openly my feelings of frustration, anger, love, and lust for Hope. Some analysts, such as Gabbard (1998), believe that it is especially risky to express feelings of lust. While Gabbard may be correct as it applies to some patients, I hope to show in this book that with other patients, like Hope, the analyst's feeling response, expressed directly, is an essential part of the analysis. This is especially true of lustful feelings, which make us analysts the most uncomfortable. In order to do this kind of analysis we require an analysis of our own that yields a vital self-knowledge and character growth such that we are confident we will not act on our lustful feelings. The point I am trying to make is that our unconscious mind knows much more than we know consciously and, despite the perceived risks, responding directly from the unconscious may prove to be an aspect of analytic technique that is valuable for many patients, particularly those for whom the usual analytic technique has failed. I leave it up to the reader to evaluate this work for himself. In thinking about professional ethics, Hope wrote:

> So much of our professional ethic is built around what we shouldn't do. Love seems to be particularly prohibited between patient and analyst, at least between the lines of psychoanalytic dogma. Yet being loved and accepted just as

we are is what we all come to analysis looking for, consciously or unconsciously, while hoping that our love will not be exploited, rejected, ignored, or do harm this time. Perhaps our professional ethic also needs to be built around the question of how to love the patient and receive love from the patient in a way that each party feels safe and devoted to an analysis which seeks the truth of their experience together, with every consideration for the need the patient may have to find out difficult things in her own time. Certainly, the core of our work was the liberation of my capacity to love.

CHAPTER TWO

Trusting the Unconscious

Freud (1915) postulated that, in addition to the conscious (cs) system of thinking, which included the preconscious (pcs), which was not conscious but could easily be made conscious, there had to be an unconscious (ucs) system to explain such things as dreams and parapraxes. He believed that most of the contents of the unconscious consisted of representatives of the instincts, which he called the id, although he later recognized that part of the ego and superego were also unconscious. Modern brain imaging techniques demonstrate that our brains do, indeed, process emotional stimuli in two distinct ways, one conscious and the other unconscious, and evolutionary psychologists (Langs 1996) have called attention to how this has survival value in the Darwinian sense. Because unconscious processing of emotional stimuli does not require evaluation and judgment by the higher centers of the brain, it is much faster than conscious processing. Unconscious processing allows us to react faster to sudden danger, which would have been a great advantage to our primitive ancestors. Even more important is the fact that our sensory organs take in more stimuli than we could possibly process consciously. Without our unconscious system of processing information, the sheer volume of the data would overwhelm our conscious mind. Klein (1946), following Freud, stressed that the baby's phantasies, especially destructive phantasies, as representatives of the instincts, cause anxiety by damaging the caretaker's goodness by means of projective identification, leading to paranoid fears of the damaged caretaker. Bion (1959), accepting Klein's idea of projective identification, went on to suggest that the baby needed to project its terror into the mind of the mother, who could process the unbearable feelings and give them back to the baby in a form that was tolerable. In his view, the projective identification in this case was not destructive, but communicative. He also noted that the projective identification could go in the reverse direction, from parent to child, and thus increase the anxiety of the baby. Infant psychiatrists such as Cramer (1997) have demonstrated how a mother can project the image of her own destructive mother into the baby and then experience the baby's loving advances as hostile. It is to be expected that such a baby would then fear that its love was destructive. Analysts are also in a position where they can project into the patient.

Bion (1967) recommended that an analyst get into a state of mind he called "reverie," eschewing memory and desire so as to intuit whatever is new in the session. He believed that our minds need and seek the truth, the way our bodies need and seek food and water. To me that means that no matter how "resistant" the patient, there is always a healthy part of the patient talking softly or in code, trying to communicate the truth to us. Our patients, in their unconscious, always know the truth of their own experience, even if they are afraid or unable to put into words.

I am not convinced of the arguments used to support the concepts of a death instinct and especially of inborn destructive envy. I believe that what appears to be destructive is actually an attempt to get the supplies that are needed, whether food, love, protection, comfort, or understanding. No matter how much the patient's behavior is experienced as destructive and attacking, it always has an aspect in which it is an attempt to communicate the patient's truth. Most important, both authors believe that the unconscious has access to the truth about our experience and the experience of the world in which we live.

～

Hope adds: While I do not believe in a death instinct, I do believe in basic defect in human nature, the consequences of which are pervasively evident in our world. There obviously is something like destructive envy, selfishness, or lust for power at work—an unwillingness to surrender to something higher than self-interest. It is not easy for us to learn love. As Bion (1984b) and others have observed, the mechanism of projective identification (behavior which produces, often unconsciously, a desired transfer of a mental or even physical effect to the other) can be chronically directed toward evasion of the mental pain incumbent upon emotional maturation, rather than toward the hope for understanding. We might say that this type of sender has become addicted to this means of avoiding painful states, just as an alcoholic is addicted to his bottle as a means of tuning out. Moreover, we may presume that the chronic sender of pain enjoys this process in some way, as the alcoholic his high, until the ruinous end of this evasive approach to life looms. Of course, in both cases, the *habit* of evading painful states could precisely be founded upon never having had the experience of another willing to "suffer" and mentally metabolize our unprocessed pain in an effort to understand our experience and to communicate that understanding. The analyst's capacity and willingness to suffer the patient's painful projections thoughtfully, without retaliation or withdrawal (Winnicott 1982), can make all the difference in facilitating each individual's inborn potential to choose to love back. Sometimes it may require *long* suffering on the part of the analyst, as in my stubborn case. There are innumerable factors, of course, which impact our inborn potential to grow in love, and some people are more fortunate than others in genetic temperament and environmental conditions that favor the development of trust and reciprocal love. Nonetheless, I do not see a way around the requirement for each one of us to make a personal choice, early or late, and daily, to accept or reject the personal privation attendant upon emotional/spiritual maturation and the growth of love. Moreover, we may fail our patients who are not inclined in this direction by neglecting to interact vigorously at some point with their commitment to self-deception.

Thus, I do not believe that we can say that the unconscious is only truth-seeking in its function, nor that if the analyst (parent, society, etc.) is good enough, most of us will grow into persons who are deeply concerned for our neighbor as well as for ourselves. This view places too much responsibility on the environmental side of the equation, and not enough on the self. As I see it, there is a war between deception and truth in the mind, conscious and unconscious, which requires a choice to pursue truth. I do agree with Dr. Marcus that the truth-telling function of the unconscious is always seeking a conscious hearing, but it does battle with an equally insistent impulse to evade the high cost of love. Mature love, as T. S. Eliot (1971) so beautifully conceived it, is very costly yet yields peace of mind:

> A condition of complete simplicity
> (Costing not less than everything)

That said, Dr. Marcus's staunch belief in goodness was a particularly good match for me, as I felt myself to be bad behind it all, *and* wished to be good! His capacity to suffer my abusive behavior toward him without concluding, even covertly, that I was bad, freed my goodness and love. Every person deserves and needs this chance.

～

Dr. Marcus continues: In my daily practice of psychoanalysis, I often forget how much my work depends upon the fact that I trust the patient's unconscious. As noted above, I assume that no matter how great is the resistance, the patient's unconscious is always attempting to find a way to communicate the truth of their unprocessed emotional experience. If I can receive the communication, I can process it so as to give it meaning. Once processed and given meaning, it is no longer toxic and can be returned to the patient, who can use it for growth. I also assume that in performing this function for the baby part of the patient's mind, I have done something the parents were unable to do. Often it becomes apparent that not only could the parents not detoxify their baby's unbearable emotional experience, they used their baby as a container for their own unprocessed unbearable infantile experience, so the baby ended up with a double dose of what was terrifying. Such babies, as adults, come to the analysis with terror that they have spent a lifetime trying to understand.

In addition, I trust that the patient's unconscious knows when my interpretations are valid, and will find a way to keep me informed. I could not work without the help of the patient's unconscious, because it is the patient and *only* the patient who can know if I have correctly understood him or her. This confirmation or nonconfirmation will generally come in code or in a dream that is always present if I search for it.

What about the analyst's unconscious? How much can it be trusted? This is an individual matter that can only be learned from experience. I can describe my own experience, which may have general validity, but each analyst can only learn from personal experience. My own experience is that whenever I respond from my unconscious, no matter how risky it may feel at the time, it is always in touch with the patient in an important way. This has proved to be true whether I understood what my unconscious was saying or not.

It ought not surprise us that the analyst's unconscious would be in touch with the patient's unconscious. It is hard to believe it could be otherwise when we have such intimate contact. One question that arises is this: How does an analyst know when the unconscious is speaking? For me it occurs in many ways, but it always has three characteristics: (1) it occurs suddenly for no apparent reason, (2) it comes as a surprise, and (3) it seems to be unrelated to what is going on in the room at the time. Common unconscious experiences that I have had include seeing beautiful colors, hearing music, remembering a scene from a movie or a book, remembering a joke, hearing the patient say something they have not actually said, and daydreams of all sorts. When whatever our unconscious has to say seems unrelated to the actual session, it feels very risky to use it because only the patient can know if it has anything to do with them at that time. Nevertheless, I hope that this book will show that the risk is well worth taking.

~

CHAPTER THREE

The Analyst

I was born in 1924 in Brooklyn, New York, the only child of first-generation Jewish American parents. My father was also an only child of parents who came to this country in the 1880s from an area of Europe that was sometimes German and at other times Austrian. My father's mother died shortly before I was born. His father, my grandfather, was a vigorous man who worked until a week before his death at the age of ninety-three. He lived with us until I was eleven, and he and I were very close. Despite being over seventy-five years old at the time, he bought a 1926 Hupmobile, which he washed and polished every Sunday.

My mother had five older sisters and a baby brother. Her parents also came to this country in the late 1880s, probably from some place in Eastern Europe. I remember her parents well, but even though I must have been seven or eight when they died, I was "protected" by not being told of their death. My mother was a beautiful woman who often had to take to her bed with headaches. These bouts of headaches were called "nervous exhaustion" and usually occurred after she had spent several days nursing a sick relative. Everyone called her a saint. She was subject to bouts of depression and was always anxious. I loved her dearly and learned to detect her moods as soon as I saw her so as to be careful not to hurt her. Despite my efforts, I was often made to feel guilty. A most painful example occurred when at the age of three or four, I asked my mother for a sibling. She told me that she could not have any more children because I had torn her so badly when I was born. It was my fault that I did not have a brother or a sister.

My father, while sickly as a boy, became a star football and baseball player in high school. I have fond memories of his teaching me to play these sports as well as teaching me to shoot a rifle. I became a good athlete also, but I was never allowed to play competitive sports in high school because of my mother's fears that I would get hurt. Despite her fears, I managed to play sand-lot football and playground softball, which were actually more dangerous, but this had to be kept from my mother. My father was a "good" man, well loved by everyone. He started in a menial job and rose to be regional manager of some thirty stores in a large retail chain. We were very well-to-do until the Depression, when my father lost his small fortune in the stock market. He never fully recovered from this blow, but despite the hard times, he managed to support his family so that we always had shelter and enough to eat.

Like my mother, he was also very sensitive. One winter day during the worst of the Depression, when I was nine or ten, my mother was wishing she could afford a fur coat to protect her against the cold. I told her not to worry, that I would buy her a fur coat when I was older. My father said nothing, but the next day my mother told me privately how much I had hurt him and had activated his peptic ulcer. I learned early that expressing myself often hurt the people I loved and left me feeling guilty. I learned to be careful, especially about expressing love. I never consciously chose to become a physician, although I "knew" when I was very young that I was meant to be one. There is a family story that when I was three years old, my mother went into the hospital to have pelvic surgery. My father refused to take her home on the day she was to be discharged, insisting that she was not well. That night she had a pulmonary embolism and the intern on call who saved her life was named Donald Marcus. I heard this story many times, and I have no doubt it had a lot to do with my unconscious choice to become a physician.

Despite my early interest in medicine, it is not likely I would have been able to go to medical school had it not been for World War II and a lot of good fortune. When I became eligible for the draft in August 1942, I applied for and was accepted into the Navy V-12 program. This meant I would be allowed to finish my premedical studies. In July 1943 I was inducted into the Navy and sent to the Massachusetts Institute of Technology for the last two semesters of premedical studies. I was then told that while I was considered an acceptable applicant, there was no place for me in medical school at that time or in the foreseeable future. I was offered the choice of becoming a hospital corpsman, through which there was an unlikely possibility of going to medical school, or going to deck officer's school, where I would get a commission as an ensign in the Navy. Despite the allure of an officer's commission to a nineteen-year-old, I chose the outside possibility of medical school and was sent to boot camp and then on to the Oakland Naval Hospital as a hospital corpsman third class. Each week a group of about thirty corpsmen was shipped out, usually to go with the Marines, fighting on the South Pacific islands. By good fortune, I was allowed to remain in the hospital for seven months until January 1945, at which time I was assigned to the medical school of Indiana University at Bloomington, Indiana. The Navy ended its program in December 1945, and my good fortune continued as the GI Bill paid my way through the rest of medical school.

Having loved California, both while in the Navy and also when we lived in Los Angeles for two months when I was eleven, I chose Los Angeles for my internship and stayed on for residency in internal medicine, which I had been led to believe was the pinnacle of medical specialties. It was during this residency that I came to realize how much of medicine had an underlying psychiatric basis, and I switched to psychiatry, much to the displeasure of all my teachers who thought highly of my ability as an internist. It was the first time I can remember openly defying parental figures. My father was especially disappointed, commenting, "I thought you were going to be a doctor."

After only four months of psychiatric residency, I was recalled to active duty during the Korean War, this time as a physician. Again, I had the good fortune to remain in this country. Following my discharge, I simultaneously continued my residency in psychiatry and began my analytic training. In 1961, I was graduated from the Institute for Psychoanalytic Medicine of Southern California, which later became the Southern California Psychoanalytic Institute and has now been merged into the New Center for Psychoanalysis. While my analytic training and training analysis were useful, I sensed that I needed to get to deeper levels of my mind. Accordingly, I began a ten-year Kleinian analysis in 1969. This analysis prepared me for my encounter with Wilfred Bion.

I began to work analytically using Bion's recommendations at the same time that I was getting weekly supervision from him. It soon became clear to me that working "without memory and desire," in a state of reverie, was an effective way for me to work, allowing my patient and me to make discoveries about what was unknown. It especially made it possible for me to use my unconscious to intuit what was newly emerging. Working without memory and desire permitted me to be fully present in my body and emotionally close to my patient, which in turn required me to devise theories which fit the experience that I was actually having in the consulting room at that moment. Self-destructive behavior, which I might once have interpreted as evidence of the death instinct, I came to recognize as self-protective, the use of destructiveness in the service of the life instinct. I came to believe that for many people—perhaps most—physical survival was not as important as survival of the self or soul or spirit. In addition, I had many experiences (Marcus 1997) which led me to believe that we all knew more about each other than could be explained by the usual known science. By getting into a state of reverie, I find that I am open to receiving information that I call intuition. Sometimes this information seems quite uncanny. Most important, memories and desires tend to saturate the mind, diminishing the room available for new experience. Patients were quick to notice the extra space available when I worked in this manner. They would comment on the large space in the room and in my mind, which they felt welcomed all aspects of their personality. Other patients would note with surprise that they had just expressed something they had not mentioned to a previous analyst. (In several instances, I was the previous analyst.) Creating this large, safe space permitted new and surprising experience to occur.

The Initial Contact

I first met Hope when she was a student in a clinical case conference that I was teaching. She was an attractive woman, without children, in her mid-forties. I liked her immediately because she had ideas of her own, which she was not afraid to express. Shortly after the case conference ended, she came to me for individual supervision, which went well, except that on two occasions, I made comments that were hurtful to her. When she called it to my attention, I was able to see her point and to apologize. This particular interaction appeared to be very important to her, as though it were quite unexpected. After a few months of supervision, she asked to enter analysis with me. I was pleased, feeling that I could be of considerable help to her in her personal exploration, just as I was pleased when she had asked for individual supervision. She began her analysis by telling me that her training analysis had helped in many ways, but in the end had failed to do the job because her analyst seemed to be hiding his true self, and she could not make what felt like real contact with him. She believed that an analysis could only be successful if both parties' true selves made intimate emotional contact. Since I was in complete agreement with her, I thought that a successful analysis was a real possibility.

It is worth noting that from the very beginning, Hope was able to tell me what she needed. I was very fortunate to have a patient like Hope who was able to help me so much.

~

CHAPTER FOUR

The Patient

In spite of it being my idea initially to write collaboratively about our work together, I wrestled with some interior objections to giving up the privacy of my analysis. I was also concerned to protect the privacy of people who came to play a part in my story, as it unfolded in the work with Dr. Marcus. We have done what we can to protect others' identities in the narrative. I decided to go ahead with the project because of my sense that our work had resulted in profound changes in me, which continue still. As Dr. Marcus felt that I was a gift to him, I believe that he was a gift to me sent to reveal the truth of my condition and to teach me love. I hope that the telling of our work will bear fruit for many.

History

It was with joy and terror that I found myself a candidate in psychoanalysis at the age of forty-five. Of my siblings, only my brother had attended college, but he dropped out after one year, and here I was with a Ph.D. and wanting more yet! If I could have articulated the unconscious dread I felt, it might have said, "How dare you!"—something I had heard from my grandmother when she found me curled up with a book one Saturday afternoon instead of doing housework. My father, too, had expressed disapproval when I left a "secure" secretarial job at twenty-one to make my first try at college. My family had struggled financially, but we always had shelter, food, and good basic schooling. We were truly poor only in expressions of love and caregiving. I was the fourth of six children, and the fourth in five years, the third girl. I don't have any photos of my mother holding me. I think she must've been completely exhausted and overwhelmed when I was born. When the doctor called my father to say that he had a healthy baby girl, he said, "You can keep her!" and slammed down the phone. This was a story my mother retold, in a humorous vein. Another story was how everything went downhill when I was born. My father started drinking in earnest again. We all suffered along with my dad from the ravages of his violent alcoholism and mood swings. My mother was devoted to keeping us together, working long hours as a waitress, but had little left over when she'd return home exhausted late in the evening. She often spoke harshly to us then. Her great vivacity and sense of fun wore down under the years of abuse, but her faith sustained her through countless sorrows. She and my father were star-crossed lovers, like Stella and Stanley Kowalski in Tennessee Williams's A Streetcar Named Desire (1951). They were passionately attached yet cruel to one another. Without words, they communicated to us the deep conviction that to love is dangerous. I mulled over the words of my mother's favorite song, "Smoke Gets in Your Eyes." She sang it often. It tells the story of a passionate love lost through betrayal; its message is that to give your heart is young and foolish, leaving you open to cynical ridicule and humiliation. We all loved her desperately in spite of the unpredictable, cruel rejection she expressed toward us, especially when she was exhausted and drank at night. My mother died of cancer as I left for my second, successful attempt at college at twenty-two, and my dad died three years later, suffering a fatal heart attack. Although I was unable to grieve at the time, the tragedy of their painful, traumatic relationship and unfulfilled lives remained a burden for all of their children to carry and to work out in our own way and time. This is the need I still carried in my late forties when I entered analysis with Dr. Marcus.

I began to seek help for myself as my first marriage came apart during graduate school. Although my husband had been instrumental in leading me to my vocation, he had strangely lost passion for the field of psychology and dropped out of his studies. As I advanced in my studies, he seemed to not love me anymore and I became depressed. One night he brought a friend over, and as we were all enjoying the evening on our roof, my husband went downstairs for something. His "friend" grabbed me and kissed me, and I found myself helpless against his outrageous advance. It was as though I were wearing a sign inviting him to make a pass! I suddenly became aware that I felt starved for love. I eventually fled the marriage only to find myself caught up in a series of unsatisfying, brief involvements.

Upon my introduction to psychoanalysis in a graduate case seminar, I found myself thinking, "That's what I need! But how can I get it?" I was fortunate to receive a combined five years of low-fee psychoanalytic therapy from two analysts as I finished my Ph.D., but I continued to make poor choices in love. I left the first treatment about the end of the third year, shortly after introducing dreams of the analyst in which I saw her as an enticing, lewd mother-person. I can still see her shaking her head in agreement with me and smiling when I suggested that the dreams seemed to be devaluative. I don't recall any attempt on her part to engage the experience with me and was left feeling that something very bad and shameful was emerging through which I would sully our good relationship.

My moving away for internship interrupted the second treatment, though I actually traveled back by train every Saturday for a double session for over a year. Still, I believe I made a flight into health as I ended this treatment, too. I remember traveling to one Saturday session through a blizzard. Arriving late at the station, I called breathless to ask if I could still come. My analyst surprised me with an extra measure of kindness when he asked what kind of tea I would like to have waiting for me. When he presented the tea to me, however, it was a clumsy job and spilled everywhere. I was quite disappointed and felt the kindness to have been spoiled. I share this incident because it sticks in my mind, while I remain unclear about why I actually ended that treatment. I wonder, as in my third treatment, whether it had to do with sensing that he did not understand that it was not the tea per se that I needed, but an intimate analytic relationship with him. I learned many years later that this analyst had left his lovely wife to marry a patient who'd become pregnant during their affair. I think now that perhaps my unconscious apprehended a lack of safety with him. My father, in his alcoholic degeneration, had molested two of my sisters and devalued and ridiculed my other sister when she began dating, not to mention beating my mother in paranoid jealous rages. I needed an analyst who could unlock my love and passion, but with whom I could feel absolutely safe. I understood none of this then, of course, but my unconscious did!

In spite of the incomplete endings, I believe the love and care I received in these beginning treatments benefited me deeply. I soon became part of a community of faith in which I experienced my first real sense of the material, emotional, and spiritual nourishment a family and friends can provide. I completed my Ph.D. and began my clinical and teaching career. I seemed to do well enough at it, yet I lacked confidence. I continued to struggle with anxiety and difficulties in self-regulation, such as in the areas of sleep and eating habits. I craved sugar. Toward the end of my marriage and the year following the divorce I began to use wine to medicate myself at night for sleep and discovered that I could not regulate that usage either. Unconsciously, I believe, I chose to live with roommates and in communities where drinking was uncommon, and then enjoyed a very long reprieve from its lure.

Five years later, I was delighted to find myself in a position to undertake a full psychoanalysis, which lasted more than a decade. It was through this analyst's very significant contribution to my healing that I chose and was chosen by my present husband, my own true love. I had belatedly realized with some sense of shock that one chooses a spouse on the basis of character, not just passion! By character I refer in part to that demonstration over time that one truly is the beloved. The analysis began to bog down, however, as I became very troubled in the work. In fact, I was in a kind of tantrum state, reminiscent of the one that followed my younger brother's birth when I was four. He was the long-awaited second boy, and my tantrums endured through much of his first year. I remember my father taking my siblings and me away on the train for what seemed a long visit with relatives, leaving my mother and infant brother home alone. I was too young to think about how I felt, but my sense is that I imagined them in love, while I was being sent away for my very bad behavior, which included pooping my pants, head-banging, and holding my breath until I fainted! Clearly, I was a demanding and desperate child! None of my siblings behaved so badly. I remember my mother drawing away from me in fear during this period. Now I conclude that she probably identified me with my father in his rages, and also with her own mother who beat her children. It occurs to me, too, that perhaps she saw her own passionate self in me. During that visit away I sustained a head injury, falling down a steep hill into a tree in pursuit of my older siblings. I remember feeling surprise and joy when my mother appeared at my hospital crib side. She gave me a pretty tin bank in the shape of a globe. However, I saw on her face a familiar expression, hard to articulate even now. She was certainly alarmed, but she also conveyed a certain hopelessness about me, a demanding, accident-prone child from whom she could not extricate herself.

I believe it is a testament to the good work we had done in this analysis that I was able to tolerate experiencing this tantrum with my analyst, rather than running away again. Moreover, I felt the right to bring my complaint to bear on him! The trouble was, I couldn't articulate, even to myself, the nature of my complaint except that I felt I was banging my head on a hard object, which put me in mind of those tantrums at the age of four. But I did feel sure that the jam we were in was not my fault alone, and this was a great liberation for which I am forever grateful! I do remember, preceding this breakdown, a very loving phase in which I wrote a passionate poem to my analyst. I don't remember him having much response. Also, I remember telling him something about wishes I had to seduce him, and I remember him making a comment about my wanting to "ruin" him.

As I continued to be angry, I remember my analyst telling me that "[we had] to go through this." He indicated, too, that "[he could] take it"! That bothered me. It was like he was saying that he could bear up under my abusive behavior. But I didn't want to be abusive. I wanted him to help me understand why I was so mad at him. Eventually, I found the gumption to tell him that I didn't feel we should go on this way, and that it felt destructive. I would say now that it felt like a repetition, in which I was cast as the "bad one." In the unconscious drama, my analyst was long-suffering and good, just as I saw my mother during my time of tantrum and, by the way, my first analyst at the time of the dreams! However, my good mother turned me over to my father, who "cured" me by enlisting my siblings together with him in the most painful, abusive ridicule when I was encopretic and beside myself in tantrum agony. They called me "Shitty Pants." Unwittingly, my good analyst seemed to be abandoning me to that same bad internal object through his apparent unwillingness or incapacity to take on some of the fault for the mess occurring between us. Moreover, as with my mother, I could not tell what he really felt and thought about me, whether he was able to find any love and goodness in me at all as I brought the tantrum.

How I Chose Dr. Marcus

I first met Dr. Marcus in a case seminar late in my analytic training. I had just finished a seminar in which I had received what felt like a scathing evaluation. Peering at me over the rim of his glasses, the instructor-analyst had said something like, "You have your own ideas, but in this case the subject was Klein!" I was inclined to agree with him that I had been horribly impertinent to introduce another perspective (the relational) into the class discussion.

I had heard of Dr. Marcus from a friend who was in analysis with him and to whom I had with some trepidation confided that my analysis was in trouble. She thought he might be good for me. I was intrigued by her description of him as someone with a lot of "space" around him, to whom you could bring anything and with whom a lot could happen! Somehow, though, he didn't seem like a realistic possibility for me. I think it was the anxiety that jealousy could erupt between me and others with whom both he and I already had a close connection, such as the friend who had recommended him to me. Jealousy had been a volatile mixture between my parents, and between my siblings and me. My mother always told me I had "jealous thumbs" (thumbs which turn up). It is especially telling, in this light, to remember a comment I made recently to the friend who initially recommended me to Dr. Marcus, now these seven years following termination. Something came up about the difficulty of sharing an analyst and I found myself saying that I felt with Dr. Marcus something of what I experience of God's love, that he loves each of us as if we were his only one. How lovely, to not be burdened by jealousy at last!

That first day in the case seminar I found myself indeed experiencing space. Not only was the office huge, but also I spied a book on Dr. Marcus's desk on some relational topic! He seemed very relaxed and welcoming, sitting with his legs and person open. I felt quite excited by his suggestion that we wait to comment on the case until we had registered a distinct feeling or other experience from which we could speak! As the case seminar went on, though, I often felt he did not like me as much as the other candidates (I almost said "girls," of which there were four in my family, the other three having been objects of my father's lust!). Their presentations seemed so beautiful compared to mine. How could you help falling in love with them?

I don't remember my state of mind in seeking supervision with Dr. Marcus following the case seminar. I suspect I felt scared that he would be disappointed it wasn't one of the other candidates who chose him (although they very well may have!). But he seemed quite pleased to be asked! One day shortly into the supervision I was feeling quite depressed and found myself telling him that my analysis was bogged down and that I was leaving it. I believe I said that I didn't feel I could reach to my analyst's real self, that I could not tell what he really thought and felt. I felt like I was banging my head on a hard object and was reacting with a kind of tantrum.

After I revealed the stalemate of my analysis to Dr. Marcus, I wondered aloud why I was telling him about this personal matter. My remembrance is that he said, "Perhaps it is because you are interested in entering analysis with me." I was shocked and I thought, if I did not say, "Is that a possibility?" I imagined it would be against the rules. It was the first of many experiences to come in which I learned that pretty much nothing was against the rules in analysis with Dr. Marcus so long as the relationship was focused on finding the truth of our experience together. Also, no experience was barred as long as . . . it's hard to find the right word. I was going to say so long as the experience together remained in the mental realm, but that's not quite true because physical experiences were allowed, too. In fact, he often said that his emotional experiences with me usually began as a physical sensation in his body. So the physical was admissible, as long as we did not act on our impulses. Then again, when I needed it, he was able to participate passionately with me in verbal dramatizations, to be real! We spoke the unconscious spontaneously, as it were. Dr. Marcus regarded any experience as grist for the mill and was rock solid in his commitment to doing analysis. I found that I could feel safe with him, and free.

CHAPTER FIVE

~

The Analysis

It quickly became apparent to me that Hope needed to express herself in a poetic fashion, by means of her own poetry, the poetry of others, or the words of a song. On occasion, she even sang to me to express her deepest feelings.

In retrospect, the analysis can be divided into two phases, the first lasting four years and two months in which we got to know each other and to feel safe with each other, and were able to make our way through the stalemate she had met with in her previous treatments. A termination phase lasting three months ensued, during which dramatic new work emerged for which the dissolution of the stalemate had been preparatory and essential.

Before presenting some clinical vignettes, I will try to give an overall picture of the way the analysis went. Because she was able to express her deepest feelings poetically and in song, it encouraged me to try to be poetic in return. Once when the words of a song kept obtruding into my awareness during her session, I dared to sing the song to her, despite my poor singing voice. The song's words functioned as a beautiful interpretation, and, since the analysis deepened, I took that as evidence that risks were acceptable.

During the first couple of years, she complained a lot about my style in that she had to complete interpretations for herself. She felt that she was forced to work much too hard. Perhaps the worst thing that went on was that I seemed to hurt her with many of my interpretations, which often seemed clumsy. At times, it got so bad that she thought she would have to quit. She encouraged me to get supervision to find out why I continued to hurt her. When the supervisor I wanted was on vacation, I turned to my dreams. I learned that my patient reminded me of one of my daughters, the one who exerted the most pressure on me to become the kind of father she needed. As I became aware that I was enacting something with my patient, I was able to diminish it, and my patient was able to notice how valuable it was that I had been a "bad enough" parent for her. There were many sessions in which she continued to complain about how poor my work was and how another analyst we both knew would have done it better. Just as I was beginning to wonder if she was right, and began to question whether I was failing her, she would phone me to apologize, telling me that she was sorry to have to hurt me so and that she knew our work together was very good for her.

Patient's Comment: My demand for "complete interpretations" was clearly a defense against the necessary analytic *experience* emerging between us. Even then, I did not like an intellectual, airtight interpretive style. Airtight, know-it-all interpretations keep the analyst and patient far apart. However, I think I needed to test whether Dr. Marcus would construe my criticism and demanding manner as bad—whether I was safe to become more vulnerable in interactive experiencing. At the same time, I was enacting a necessary complaint against my parents' incapacity to think about my tantrum behavior, and my feelings in general. Indeed, many childhood photos show me with a furrowed brow and distressed expression. Perhaps I was trying to think about my own confused experience.

This first period of her analysis presented her with the opportunity to relive and come to terms with her relationship with her mother, to eventually become reconciled with her mother's shortcomings, and to recapture her deep love for her. The depth and elaboration of this result in her life, however, did not become apparent until some time after termination, emerging even as we worked on this book together. Then, one day, after four years and two months of analysis, she announced that she thought it was time for her to end the treatment. The ending date for the analysis was set for three months after her announcement. While it seemed much too short to me, this deadline proved to be a stimulus that allowed and encouraged us to do the crucial, important work of reaching past her (our?) fears to her sexual passion and need for surrender.

The First Phase of the Analysis
(Learning to Trust Each Other)

We agreed to begin work at four times per week, and Hope chose to use the couch from the start. The only notes I have on the first few months of the analysis are that she began to feel more alive, both to herself and to me. In the fourth month of the analysis, she brought in a dream from which she had awakened in a panic. She was choking and could not breathe. In the dream, there was a man, perhaps a couple, who were vampires. Her associations led her to recognize her unconscious fear that I was a vampire who, like her parents, would suck the life out of her. It appeared to be a reaction to her belief that I had helped her become more alive, but it also seemed to be an unconscious memory of her infantile experience.

Analyst's Comment: There are many ways to think about this dream, but my preference is to think of it as a memory of what actually occurred in infancy, as well as a fear that this same infantile experience would happen again with me if she dared to reclaim her active, vital, curious, and creative self. She feared that I, like her parents, needed to drain her vitality so I could live.

Patient's Comment: I find this a beautiful interpretation now, though at the time I remember feeling confused by it, perhaps because it was so different from what I expected. I imagine I expected to be pronounced guilty of projecting the vampires' insatiable thirst into the vampire couple.

Slowly, she got me to understand that she needed me to hold her in such a way that she felt safe, but not so tightly that she could not get away when she felt she needed to. Once, after a difficult session in which she was very critical of me, she left me a message that I took as advice and supervision: "Don't let me push you away." There were many sessions in which she was very critical of me, leaving me feeling guilty and wondering if I had, in fact, behaved as badly as my guilt would suggest. Almost invariably, following these sessions, she would leave me a message letting me know that she knew our work together was good and helpful. These messages were very reassuring to me, relieving my guilt and giving me the courage I needed to continue the work.

On one occasion, Hope had twice made a slip about "our Friday" session (which we did not have), and I suggested that even though she had given up her Tuesday session, that we still seemed to have four weekly sessions. In the next session, she told me that she felt we had actually had a session on Tuesday, the session she had given up. She had very much liked my interpretation that she had had a session on Friday because she felt it was original and surprising. I suggested that she now seemed to be having five sessions per week instead of the three we were actually having. She agreed and then went on to tell of creative work she had been doing which had been "spit on by her supervisor." She said, "I feel a deep connection with you, something like an umbilical cord between our guts. I feel that you 'get' me—feel me. I am beginning to relax. However, I also feel that sometimes you don't get me." She went on to tell the story her mother laughingly told of her birth: Her arms were too long and thin, and she was all red, "like a chicken." She was always trying to get her mother to value and love her, but it was like hitting her head against a wall. In fact, she actually did bang her head against the wall as a little girl, perhaps as a way of talking about her experience. I noted to myself that in addition to experiencing me as a new, good mother, it appeared she needed to experience me as a bad mother, whom she could correct or change, making me into a mother who understood her and could see her beauty. Much later, she was able to tell me that one of the things that had helped her most was that I had been a "bad enough mother."

One day, as she was leaving my office, she said, "I love you." That night, she had a dream in which she and her husband no longer loved each other, and he had another woman. The dream was causing her to feel panicky. Her associations were to how much better she and her husband were getting along, especially in expressing their love. She also told me how her mother would make her feel guilty by constantly telling her she was bad and projecting her own guilt into her. I suggested that she felt guilty about expressing her loving feelings toward me in the previous session, and then began to punish and abuse herself as her mother had done to her. She responded that she had been eating too much candy and drinking too much wine, which is a way that she does abuse herself. She went on to talk about how dangerous it was to love, because when she does, her internal mother attacks and punishes her. That night, she left me a message that she was no longer feeling guilty and panicky, but was feeling sad about the way she abuses me. She said she felt very connected to me and ended with a sincere "thanks." The next day, she told me of her worry about whether I would be able to help her deal with her vicious internal attacking mother, who rejects her love and responds by attacking her and her love. I told Hope that I thought she had been attacking me much as her internal mother attacks her to give me an idea of what it was like, and also to test me out. She replied that we were engaged in a life-threatening enterprise, like something she'd read about as a child where a doctor tried to lure a tapeworm to come up and out a child's opened mouth while she sat very still. There'd been a photo of the procedure in the book, as well. She feared the tapeworm would get frightened and go back inside her and choke her. She talked of her fear of having an asthmatic attack, which might kill her, in the office. She wondered if I would be strong enough to cope with the vicious part of her that was like a moray eel.

⌒

Analyst's Comment: I recall my anxiety as I became aware of the dangerous task ahead. As Hope reclaimed her capacity to love, she and I would have to confront a formidable opponent in the form of her "moray eel." It occurs to me now that the concept of projective identification could explain my anxiety, and it might have been useful to interpret that she needed me to feel how deathly frightened she felt. She needed to know that I could feel the anxiety and still continue with the life-threatening enterprise of her analysis.

⌒

There followed a number of sessions which she described as "searching for sadism in me." When she could not find it, she felt safe. If I were not going to "project my sadism into her," as my hidden agenda, she would have the opportunity to "own her own sadism." It also made her feel safe that I did not "masochistically accept her projections into me." I was able to find an opportunity to call her attention to her confusion, in which, like her mother, she believed that her love was sadistic. She was very appreciative for this clarification and said, "I love you." Immediately, she began to feel embarrassed. I made some intervention that she felt did not allow her to stay with her feelings of love and embarrassment. She said she was hurt and angry. I told her that I could see how my comment could have that effect, and she was much relieved, having expected me to accuse her of being too sensitive, as was always done in her family.

In the next session, she told me that she thought I was transparent rather than opaque; that I had no hidden agenda and would not give her poison along with food for thought. Her mother called her pig in French with some disgust, "Cochon!" She believed this label and felt like a pig or a tapeworm, always wanting more sweets.

⌒

Patient's Comment: I had no idea my food cravings as a child signaled desire for loving attention. I had no idea what it meant to be satisfied. Dr. Marcus's thoughtful approach to my anxieties felt original and satisfying.

⌒

A few sessions later, she brought in a dream in which she was missing her husband because he had left her very coldly. He took her back but he was cold and fat. He said, "You could at least cut down to one analytic session per week." She said she had been feeling hungry, was eating a lot of sweets, and was afraid of getting fat. I interpreted that this "fat" her wanted to separate us. She replied that she was in danger and could die. I said that I thought there was a dangerous part of her that threatens to kill her. She told me that she was angry with me because I had not attended a scientific program on enactments that she had attended. Then she told me that she could not see how she was reacting to any coldness of mine. I called her attention to two missed sessions because of the Thanksgiving Day holiday. She reacted to my interpretation with great disdain and dismissiveness. She was aware of the disdain in her voice, telling me that it was how her parents treated her. She felt she had to take in fat, cold, disdainful parents as a way of protecting the elemental part of her.

That night, Hope left me a phone message, telling me how sad she felt that she had treated me so badly in the session. She knew I didn't deserve it, just as she had not deserved it when she was little. She related it to the hurt she had to bring in. She was sad that she could not bring in the feelings without being disdainful of me. She said she would try not to behave that way. I very much appreciated the phone message because I had been feeling quite bad. The call let me know that I was, indeed, doing good work. She came in smiling for her next session and asked to use the phone. I hesitated for a moment, and then asked her about it. She replied that her husband was going to the airport, and she wanted to warn him about all the traffic she had encountered as she drove by. I agreed to let her use the phone, and she then made a brief call, suggesting to her husband that he get to the airport early.

Once on the couch, she told me that she was hurt that I had hesitated to let her use the phone. She asked why I had hesitated. I reminded her of the two mischievous, destructive little girls who had appeared in one of her recent dreams. I told her that I was concerned, wanting to protect her analysis against something potentially destructive. She replied that the older girl was destructive but that the little girl was hurt. She sounded very hurt, and I told her that I was sorry I had hurt her. I realized I could have allowed the phone call and then analyzed any trouble that arose. She asked why I had done something to hurt her. I told her that I didn't know but that anxiety might have played a role, or perhaps it was part of an unconscious enactment. She continued to feel hurt and angry despite my best efforts to repair the damage.

Whatever I said seemed to increase her distress and she left the session quite distraught. After she left, I tried to figure out what we had enacted. I felt like a little girl—her—who did not do anything terrible and was trying to put things right, but all my attempts at repair were rebuffed.

Later that day, she left me a message in a cheerful voice, telling me she did not want me to struggle without some added information. Although she was distraught when she left my office, she soon realized she was not feeling bad. She was composed, gleeful, and mischievous. She told me that I was onto something about the two girls; she was out of touch with the mischievous one. In her dream, it was she who had to stop those little girls. In our enactment, I was the one whose job it was to stop the little girls from doing mischief. She was delighted to discover this mischievous little girl part of her, which she could now integrate into her personality. She recognized that it could wreak havoc between us and might even wish to get her to quit, but she was glad that I could "smell it." She wanted me to connect with that mischievous but also very lively part of her. Needless to say, I was relieved to get the phone message.

Patient's Comment: In reading this material I am deeply moved, experiencing again how Dr. Marcus does not become bitter and unforgiving toward me through the repeated attacks. I felt this in the analysis and knew it to be the truth *inside* of him, too. He is always pleased and helped by my apologies. I am able to go on with this dirty work because I am able to be of some help in spite of it all, like Charlotte the spider who could go on with the bloody business of a spider's life because she was able to be of help to Wilbur, the pig. "It lifts the life," as she said (White 1952). Also, I felt how deeply Dr. Marcus genuinely struggled with his part in the recurrent disappointing encounters. He was not busy with defensive conceptualizations in the privacy of his own mind. Most of all, he continued to delight in me!

Analyst's Response: Hope is quite right that I did not become bitter or unforgiving toward her because of her repeated attacks. She always managed to give me just enough to relieve my anxiety and to delight me. There were, indeed, recurrent disappointing encounters, but each one was resolved in a way that made me feel good, confirming my belief that Hope and I were good for each other.

I do not have notes on the next session, but she refers to it in the session that followed it. She had a dream of a man in a boat and she is in the water splashing mud on him. The man was not very attractive and not very bright. She pulled him into the water. She was afraid he would try to push her under and drown her, but he only pushed her down to her mouth, and she was not afraid. She felt I had crushed her in the previous session. She felt like a crushed baby. She brought in a broken angel made out of milkweed pods. Only a wing had been broken off, and it was repairable. She was trying to tell me how what was called her "destructiveness" was crushed as a child, but this part of her also contained her reaching out, exploring, assertive self. She said she needed to destroy me and to crush me. Could I love the "destructive" little girl self, as well as the angel? She wondered if I would still want to see her now that she was showing me her destructiveness. When I told her that I believed something good would come from our interaction, she replied that it already had. She then asked for some Scotch tape to repair the wing of her broken angel, and I was able to help her. It was a poignant moment.

This session was followed by several sessions in which she attacked me in various ways and was very happy that I could allow her to use me as she needed and did not attack her back. In a phone message, she told me that she had left my office feeling exhilarated.

Analyst's Comment: What may not be immediately apparent in the written material is the strong positive bond that was slowly forming between us. We were learning that no matter how bad things might seem, we could trust each other to find a way to repair any damage. Even though Hope experienced herself as destructive, I did not experience her that way. What she called destructive seemed to me to be a communication or an attempt to gain understanding. She had been unfairly labeled as "bad" when she was a baby and I believe she was unconsciously trying to find out why. It was very relieving and exhilarating for her that I could see something of value in her "bad" behavior. I experienced her as not bad, but good, trying to cooperate in her analysis to the best of her ability. I was not tempted to interpret her attacks on me as destructive because I chose to trust my unconscious experience rather than some intellectual theory.

CHAPTER SIX

~

I Take My First Risk

One day, she entered the room giving me a slight smile, and then lay on the couch. She began to talk about being hard on her husband, feeling she was unfair to him, especially since he is so good to her, but they talked about it, and it was okay. Then she talked about getting supervision from Dr. Z, who is very helpful. He makes complete interpretations, unlike me, who she said hardly ever makes complete interpretations. Maybe, she thought, she should be in analysis with him, but she suspected that she would complain about him too. Then, noticing one of the paintings I have on my wall, she said, "I'm glad you have your wife's paintings in your office. It makes me feel good that you can encourage her development." She spoke for fifteen or twenty minutes in this manner, and finally said she didn't know why she was talking about all these things. She then stopped, clearly expecting me to make an interpretation. There were many possibilities that would occur to any analyst, but nothing seemed new and fresh. On the other hand, while she was talking, a song kept going through my mind. I wanted to respond with something new, and as I thought about telling her of the song, I could imagine her responding in a scathing manner. Nevertheless, she had many times told me about songs in her mind which expressed her feelings exactly. I also felt that it was an opportunity that I would lose if I did not risk her potential contempt. Finally, I said, "I don't know if this song says more about me than about you, but it kept going through my mind as you were talking." And then I sang to her: "A song of love is a sad song, hi lili, hi lili, hi lo." There was dead silence. I had no idea as to her reaction, but as the silence continued, I began to think that I had really made a mess of things. I wished I had kept quiet. After what seemed like an eternity, but was probably only two or three minutes, she said, "That's the kind of song my mother always sang to me about the pain of loving." She continued about how painful it was to love her mother, who would show her some love, and when she responded, would reject her. She could remember all the songs her mother sang about the pain of loving and how she too was afraid to feel and express her love because of her fear of being rejected and hurt. I asked whether she might be feeling hurt about the week's vacation that was coming up. As we talked about this, it emerged that she was extending her vacation beyond mine and did not remember that she would be away one day that I was working. I could not find a way to interpret her forgetting, but the session had a different tone, one that was more comfortable for me, where I did not feel on guard. She, too, seemed to feel more comfortable, and when she left, she turned at the door and said in a loving manner, "It's good you brought up the matter of the sessions to be missed." She seemed to be implying that I did not need to worry. I wondered if she was also telling me that it was good I sang the song.

Analyst's Comments: There is no way to know how this session would have gone had I not sung the song. The only thing I can know is that singing the song had a powerful effect in that it touched my patient in a place that was not apparent from her words. That my unconscious mind understood what her unconscious was communicating and came up with that song as a perfect response is beyond anything I could do consciously. It served as an unusual interpretation of which I was unaware at the time I made it. Usually we use our conscious mind to formulate an interpretation of the patient's unconscious communication. In this instance, my conscious mind simply made the decision to allow my unconscious to speak directly to hers. Because of the good effect here and on other occasions, I suggest that we may want to add this to our armamentarium for use when it may be appropriate. While this session was important because it deepened the analysis, it also had the added effect of teaching me that I could, with this woman, dare to take risks by following my unconscious.

It is also the kind of session that raises many questions. Why did just that song enter my mind with such insistence that I felt I had to use it? We may never know the answer to that question, but there seems to be no questioning that when two people have a deep emotional relationship, they know much more about each other than they are aware. I believe that my unconscious mind picked up some message from her unconscious mind, and came up with a song which would connect with her at a deep level, exactly what went on between her mother and her when she was a baby.

Patient's Comment: Tears. Thank you for the song, a most beautiful interpretation which went directly to my heart. To employ the language of Stern et al. (1998), this was a "something happened" experience for me, penetrating immediately to my unconscious state, as music so often does. I think Dr. Marcus must have especially gifted *mirror neurons* that prime the brain to imitate *bodily* the internal state of the other (Siegel 2003). So often he was able to get hold of my unconscious state in a physical-emotional form. He would surprise and sometimes shock me with an observation of his own state, which accurately attuned to my unconscious state, even though I'd been consciously miles away from such awareness. He saw his own state and knew my state—*feeling-felt* (Siegel 1999). In this way I became more and more confident that I was inside him and he was inside me. I developed a sure trust that I was knowing him and he was knowing me. He was *with me* in scary places inside; in this case, the very sad feelings about ruined love.

Analyst's Response: While I may, as Hope suggests, have gifted mirror neurons, I suspect that most of us are born with an adequate supply of competent mirror neurons, but some of us have trained them better than usual. As a child, I needed to use them to maintain contact with my beautiful but depressed mother; as an analyst, it is an intrinsic part of my work that, as in this instance, has proved to be very valuable. When I dare to speak directly from my unconscious and it has a good (sometimes extraordinary) effect, it gives me more courage to do it again. That will become apparent later in this book.

The First Dream in Which the Analyst Appears Overtly

A little more than nine months into her analysis, Hope came for her session after a thirteen-day Christmas break and gave me a big smile. She had a cup of coffee in her hand and, instead of lying down, she sat down on the couch. It was very difficult to recapture this session because it was so full. She began by telling me that over the vacation, she had felt very free and had not worried. It was the best vacation she had ever had, but she said that she had hurt herself accidentally. In fact, she kept sticking herself with a knife and had a ski accident. Also, she said, she had her first transference dream: "In the dream, I was going to marry you, going to your house to spend the weekend with you, the way I did with my husband before we were married. Your wife had died. Your house was dilapidated. You were like Goofy. I sat on your lap but I got turned off. There were white rats sniffing around. You didn't seem to mind. A woman with a dog was sniffing around. I reached out to grab you and you fell back. I tried to put my arms around you but there was only air."

In her associations, she said that her destructiveness was important. She had killed off my wife. She had also had a skiing accident, which resulted in a concussion. "My husband says it's to stop the excitement I feel while skiing downhill. I'm not supposed to feel excitement. Now I realize I had the accident because of the need I have to look inward when excited, as if to keep an eye on things in case they get out of hand. Not wise when you're skiing! I don't know if you are aware how much I've changed. I don't know how it's happened. I no longer feel omnipotent. I do feel excitement, but I still believe it had nothing to do with you." I replied, "Perhaps I encourage or at least allow your excitement to emerge." She agreed with that and said something I could not recall after the session, but it caused me to interpret that her ski accident was being used as a warning to stop her excitement. When she gets excited, she tries whatever she can to stop it, even making me "Goofy."

She told of two more dreams. In one, there was a leaking nipple that was pierced (she, over the vacation, accidentally kept sticking a knife into herself). She could not remember the second dream except for the fact that she was eleven and there was a boy, six, and she wondered if she had killed the boy. Her association went to her brother, who was her mother's favorite, of whom she had been intensely jealous. He was hit and killed by a car when he was seven and she was eleven. She felt very guilty. She had many associations to the change in her and said, "Do you understand about the change? I am able to think about my own destructiveness. Both my parents were destructive. It's in my genes. I'm less critical of you. I don't know what you are doing, but you definitely don't pull away and are present." I said the dream seemed to be describing a projection onto me, like a hologram, so you can't grab it. "Yes," she replied, "that's interesting. Even in the dream, I knew you were not like that. What's so good about you is that you are always a presence. You accommodate to me on the surface, but always go back to your own way of working." She commented at this point that we both seemed to feel her excitement.

She went on to talk about the pierced nipple and her disgust at seeing a baby nursing and gone limp, "drunk at the breast." To her, the baby seemed to merge with the nipple and the breast. I said, "You get disgusted about a beautiful experience." She said, "It's like my difficulty having an orgasm." At some point in the session, after I had made a "good" interpretation, she said, "Intellectual understanding doesn't help me." I replied, "I think you're telling me that you need to have an experience with me where you can feel your excitement, your hunger for me, and express it without fear that I will pull away." She replied with some disdain, "Dr. Z would say that I only need to know what is keeping me from having the experience, but I don't feel like attacking you about it. I know there is a lot more I want you to understand, but I feel more patient with you." I replied that I could sense that and also that it felt as though we needed to reach out and grab each other but somehow couldn't quite do it. She said, "I feel I am pulling back." She then talked about the seminar that was to occur later in the morning. She said she would try to hide out of my sight.

⁓

Patient's Comment: I have to chuckle at my statement that I'm no longer omnipotent insofar as I still can't dare to give Dr. Marcus an ounce of credit! Also, my disdain toward his interpretation of my desire to have an experience together in which I can feel my excitement shows how far away I am from being able to allow such desire.

⁓

She came in the next day telling me how comfortable she felt with me and in her life. She was aware of having been comfortable in the seminar the previous day, and also aware how one of the other students who was usually very frightened in seminars also felt comfortable. She talked about how she was open to experience and was taking in her analysis with her guts. She said, "You don't seem to have any technique. You are just you." I said, "I just try to stay in contact with you." She replied, "It's your presence," but the word actually came out as a combination of presence and precious. I said, "Your slip suggests that you feel I'm precious and you are very appreciative." She began to cry and said she was deeply touched by my noticing her appreciation. "I feel very shy." I said, "This is when you learned you could be hurt." "Yes," she said, "when I open up."

I have no notes on the next session, but in the session after that, she began by telling me that she had felt disorganized in the previous session but was now recovered. She feels there has been a remarkable change in her in that she can think. She is in great pain about her attacks on me and she said that she was sorry. "It's hard to know why I'm doing so much better. Is it you or was I just ready? I'm sure it's partly you." I suggest that it's the mix between us, and she begins to cry. She talked about a married colleague from years ago, a poet, who wanted a platonic yet somehow erotic relationship with her, perhaps the relationship between an artist and his Muse, but she felt it was not appropriate and moreover frustrating. She thinks that I want her to smear me with honey to make myself delicious. "You want me to merge with you, and that's disgusting. I had said earlier in the day to a little girl patient of mine, 'You don't want to like me so you spoil me.'" My note to myself after the session was that Hope is afraid of her erotic urges to merge with me and to lick me, so she spoils me to avoid her erotic urges, her love. She makes me disgusting. She is disgusted by the baby her who would like to be asleep at the breast.

She began the next session by telling me that she felt disorganized: "I don't know what is happening. It was a good session here yesterday. I felt the seminar was very good. I liked the way you handled my disagreeing with you. It was good that you got M to talk. She is always so quiet, like a frightened bird, but you cut off R. I don't think you like her. And then your interpretation, linking the sadness to dry eyes and the snowflakes she saw left me breathless, it was so beautiful. I felt good until the session I had with an adolescent. I felt I goofed, and then began to think I'll never build a practice, I'll never make a good analyst. I really ripped myself apart. My husband helped me see how unfair to myself I was. I also became aware of how I was tearing you apart. You don't make interpretations. You only try to get at my feelings. You think all you have to do is be empathic, but I need more. You're stupid. I should have shopped around more for an analyst. I should have gone to Dr. Z. He makes interpretations. I feel bad attacking you like that, but it's the way I feel." I replied, "It's good that you feel free to say it directly to me." "It does feel good. I don't know what I did all those years with Dr. K. I know I got something but I didn't feel this free. What is that book on your shelf: Angel in Arms, Angel in Armor? I think I'd like to be an angel in arms." I replied, "I think you'd like to be an angel baby, held in my arms, like the baby asleep at the breast." She said, "It doesn't disgust me as much as it did." I said, "You want very much to be my angel baby held securely in my arms, but something stops you." She said, "In my mind, I'm ripping you to shreds. What kind of analyst are you, discarding all the work of others, and just working stubbornly in your own way, not making interpretations, making me make my own interpretations? I have to interpret my envy. Of course, there does seem to be room for me to think. I couldn't do this with Dr. K. You seem to make room for me." Then she went on to attack me further. I suggested that perhaps an internal me was attacking her back. "No," she said, "I think I was identifying with an attacked and damaged you."

She talked about her envy of me, having her for a patient, while she has difficult children and adolescents. She seemed to want me to interpret her envy, but since she already knew about that, I decided against it. She went on to talk about my wanting her to cover me with honey and lick me, and how I would enjoy that. She said she'd rather spoil me and make me disgusting. She approaches and is about ready to enjoy me, when she attacks me and makes me disgusting. She reminds me of my beautiful interpretation in the seminar, following which she began to attack me, to destroy my beauty. It feels as though I am being led to interpret envy, but again I'm not tempted because it's so obvious. Instead I say, "When you notice my beauty, you are tempted to come close and be an angel in my arms, but you get scared and spoil my beauty so you get disgusted and pull back." With scorn she said, "Where did you get the idea of your beauty?" I replied, "You said you gasped at the beauty of my interpretation." "Oh yes," she remembered, "I wanted to go right by that." Suddenly, she began to sob, and after a few minutes, she said, "It was your mentioning your beauty that made me sob. I never cried like this in my ten years with Dr. K. It feels good to cry, like an orgasm. It has relieved my tension. I feel now I'm relaxed at your breast." (It felt very sad and I began to have tears in my eyes and probably in my voice.) "My mother was beautiful but she didn't think that I or my feelings were beautiful." I said, "It was very painful to have a mother who could not appreciate your beauty and the beauty of your feelings." She said, "Not all my feelings are beautiful." I said, "I think they are." She said, "Not when I'm destructive," and I replied that I thought it might be difficult to see that even when she was calling me stupid, there was something beautiful about it, because it was out in the open. She paused, as if surprised, almost stunned, then told of a couple of her child patients, where she enjoys their attacks on her. At some point in this session, she told me of an appointment she was having later that day with a plastic surgeon to inquire about getting a face-lift. Toward the end of the session, she thanked me to express her appreciation for what she felt was a wonderful session. I replied that she might not be aware of how much she had given me. She fell silent, and I began to feel quite uncomfortable. Finally, she said, "I was able to let you give me something." As she left the room, she noticed my moist eyes and said, "Not a dry eye in the room."

〜

Patient's Comment: I was, indeed, stunned when you said that even my attacking expressions, like calling you "stupid," were beautiful because they were out in the open. My association to how I was able to enjoy my patients' attacks on me communicates how true I felt your statement to be! This interaction was definitely another "something happened" experience for me. I had been searching a long time to find someone other than Winnicott and myself who could see the creative value in destructiveness. But beauty? Wow!

It makes me smile to see myself say Dr. Marcus is lucky to have me for a patient, while I have difficult child patients. Yet there is a kernel of truth here in that I think he is fortunate to have a patient wanting to both express *and think about* her destructiveness, and I am fortunate to have an analyst who can delight in this work.

Analyst's Response: While it is apparent that Hope had found in me exactly the person she needed, someone who enjoyed her "destructiveness," it might not be so obvious that Hope, with her association to her enjoyment of her patients' attacks on her, had given me exactly what I needed.

In retrospect, I am surprised that I did not explore Hope's wish to get a face-lift. It appears to have all kinds of potential messages that I ignored.

She came in for her next session on Monday, saying, "After our good session last Thursday, I had nightmares Thursday and Friday night and didn't sleep well until last night. I'm angry that I have to get back to analysis, but I was on time." I said, "It's understandable that you're angry at me for causing you so much anxiety." She went on, "What do I want to come here for? I feel resistant. In the Thursday night dream, I was in an elevator with a man. It seemed to free-fall, then slow down, and then free-fall again. I was afraid I'd get broken into pieces and only my husband would look for me. There was a woman under the elevator trying to fix it. She didn't know what she was doing and she was taking her time. In Friday night's dream, I was in a haunted house with my husband. There were snakes in the basement, snakes with square jaws like dragons. My husband was about to fall backward and I yelled at him. This dream was not as scary as the Thursday dream, then it was better Saturday, and last night I slept well."

I suggested that the woman trying to fix the elevator sounded like a view that she often has of me. "Yes," she chuckled, "incompetent. You don't know what you're doing. You don't realize the degree of danger. I don't think you understand about primitive mental states." I said, "It's odd that it should occur the night of the good Thursday session." She said, "I think I'm tempted to fall into you and the dream is a warning threat to try to stop me. There's a song in my head. I can't remember it. Oh, now I remember. No more I love yous." She relaxed noticeably on the couch and said, "I feel relaxed as though I could fall into you. I remember about your beauty. I went to see a plastic surgeon after the Thursday session. I want a face-lift for my fiftieth birthday. There's something good about the way you work. I felt good crying hard. There was something beautiful. I think you've been talking about beauty in your paper." I said, "Until you mentioned it just now, I had not thought of it that way, but I think you may be right."

～

Analyst's Comment: Again I have allowed the face-lift to go by unexplored.

～

In the next session, she began by stating that she was late (approximately two minutes). "It's resistance. I got a phone call. I don't want to be here." As she said this, she crossed her arms and went on, "I also did want to come. I'm ambivalent. I had a dream in which I was looking at my breasts. I liked the way they look, which is unusual for me. They had lost the 'sucked out' look. The nipples were soft, not erect, but I was concerned. Viscous, cerulean blue fluid was leaking out. I asked a nurse but she was not concerned." In her associations, she said that cerulean blue is a heavenly blue. "I was your angel in arms: Blue eyes, nipples and eyes." It reminded her of Meltzer's book, *The Apprehension of Beauty* (1988). "I felt beautiful when I had tears on my face. My mother never felt I was beautiful. I want too much. It's that tapeworm." I said, "It's called a tapeworm but perhaps you were just hungry." She went on to talk about how she gets very hungry and then eats a lot as her way of managing her hunger. She mentioned new research on how the mother helps the child manage feelings, and at some point in the session, she again became critical of my technique, feeling that I was setting myself up as a good mother, as opposed to her bad mother. Again, she felt bad about attacking me. I suggested that it could also be seen as her trying to help me do a better job of giving her what she needed. It was the end of the session, and I couldn't be sure of her response to my last comment.

～

Analyst's Comment: As I think about this session, it appears that I was being invited to analyze her "badness," but it seemed old and known to both of us, so I chose to interpret her goodness that was newer and much less known.

～

In her next session, she came in complaining about what an awful day it had been and how she wanted to reclaim her fourth weekly session but was unable to do so because I did not have a time that she could use. However, she said she really just wanted to reject my offer. She began her usual attacks on my technique, my work, and me, but there was something very delightful in her attacks, and she even chuckled, continuing to attack me, saying, "You're different, you're dark, you have leathery skin. You prefer M because she's more like you. You don't like me. You don't want me. We're too different." As she was going on in what seemed to me a quite beautiful way, she said, "This is just a drunken soliloquy." I said, "Something beautiful is being called ugly." She said, "I feel sad but I'm glad I can think and talk about this. I could never do it with Dr. K." She had also talked about her parents, who didn't like her and turned away from her, and also that she felt that I couldn't and didn't like her since she was different and dramatic. According to my note, I said, "Perhaps because I don't turn away from you." In retrospect, I have no idea why I said that, but she responded, simply, "Dr. K didn't turn away."

She went on to tell me about an article in the *Los Angeles Times* about a keyhole in space, a dark space with fifteen hundred galaxies seen through the Hubble telescope. "It's very beautiful and has never been seen before. It goes to the edge of time." I said, "Your beauty can now be seen." She said, "I want to be born. I tried to be born on March 30 but then, after my mother was at the hospital, I didn't come. She had hoped I would be born on the anniversary of Roosevelt's death in April, and I complied. When the doctor called to tell my father he had a healthy little girl he said, 'You can keep her!' and hung up. This was another one of the stories my mother told laughing. It was always so confusing—why is she laughing? I want to be born. Can we give birth to me?" She said all this in a very poetic and beautiful way. She also recited a poem she had once written about having her own beach, a place with beautiful sand, and immediately attacked it, saying she was just being dramatic. I said, "You're attacking your beauty." She said, "I want to be dramatic, I am dramatic. I can hear you thinking I'm too volatile." There were other attacks on herself which I could not recall after the session, but I began to feel sad, and so I replied, "Actually, I feel quite sad," at which she burst into tears. She said, "I think of us as star and satellite. You take my light away." I said, "Perhaps you wonder if there will be the right amount of gravity between us," and she said, "I think of it as you're holding me in your arms. Will I let you do it or will I have to attack your beauty?"

Analyst's Comment: There are other ways I could have responded to Hope's comment that she could hear me thinking that she was too volatile. I chose to tell her that I was feeling quite sad because my sadness came as a surprise and seemed to be unrelated to the verbal content. I felt it came from my unconscious, and even though I had no idea what it meant, I had learned I could trust my unconscious, so I chose to let my unconscious speak to her unconscious. Her bursting into tears was the way her unconscious let me know that we had connected in a moment of meeting.

〜

In the next session, which was on a Monday, she came in berating me. "You don't know me. You don't know about violence. We are not kindred souls. I hate you. I hate to be here. I don't know why I'm here. I'm tired of analysis. There's nothing in it for me. I get nothing back. I'm sick of being an analyst. I don't have enough work. I'm not making enough money. My friends from grad school are doing better. One is a dean. I'm teaching a master's level course. I spent all weekend planning the course, eating lots of candy. I don't like the idea of being so angry with you. I don't want to feel transference with you. I feel very critical of you." I could not recall afterward exactly what she said which led to my calling her attention to how she seemed to be diminishing me. She corrected me by saying that it was a blast to keep me away from her. At this point, I began to feel sad. I told her so, and I wondered if she was keeping me distant to avoid the sad feelings that she comes in touch with when we get close. There was an uncomfortable silence. She broke it by saying, "I'm feeling very critical of you." Then she went on, "Of course, you only have half the facts. There have also been periods of my feeling very good. Even as I was driving here today, hating the drive, and you, and the analysis, I saw the trees against the sky and it seemed beautiful."

She then switched to feeling that she should come in for a fourth weekly session, but it was too difficult. She stated that she knew she should do more and went on in this vein, berating herself. I said, "There seems to be a voice berating you, complaining that you're not trying hard enough in here." She said, "It's the same with my course, although some people say I try too hard, and it is too much for the students. You'd say I should come in for a fourth session. I had five with Dr. K and I know you think I should have at least four." "Actually," I replied, "I think things are going reasonably well at three sessions per week." After a pause, she said, "I've gotten more with you in less than eleven months than I did with Dr. K in ten years. I don't know why that is." She went on to talk more about having periods of feeling okay with herself. She seemed to soften considerably. She told of a picture of herself at age seven where she has to pee but was holding it in. It's the same recently. She holds it in and barely makes it to the bathroom. Then she heaves a sigh of relief like having an orgasm. She would like more stimulation with me, things like touching and dancing. She told of a platonic affair that she is having with a colleague who has blue eyes and wondered if she was acting out

something with him that might be meant for me. I said, "They do seem some-
what parallel." "But," she said, "I give in more with him." She feels disori-
ented. They seem to know each other deeply. She lets herself go more. "Perhaps I know he finds me physically attractive. I don't think you do." She goes
on to talk about reasons for not letting herself go with me, and I have to stop
her in the middle of what she's saying because we have gone slightly over the
time for the session to end. As she leaves, she says, "Am I supposed to feel
bad about going over?" and I reply, "No."

Patient's Comment: I know the colleague referred to here, and we were
longtime good friends who did know each other deeply. I remember the brief
allure that emerged between us, but there was no platonic affair. Our boundaries were intact, and a frank talk dis-"spell"-ed us. Perhaps I was trying to
make Dr. Marcus jealous by exaggerating the matter.

Two days later, Hope began her next session with a dream in which she
was lying in bed with her back to her husband, pressed against him. At the
same time, she was hanging out the window of a brick building. She said to
her husband, "Don't push my hand out. Pull me in." It was said in a very firm
tone because she was afraid of falling. "I am feeling very critical of you. You
are not interpreting my falling dreams. I feel you're stupid, incompetent, and
slow. A lot like the way I feel about myself. I feel you are only interested in
sex. You like to have pretty women around you. You don't like heavy women.
You like M, who is pretty and thin. I don't feel you like me. You are slow. You
laugh like Goofy. Dr. Z would be faster. He'd know what I'm talking about. I
tell him he is teaching me the most about analysis. You don't seem to do or
know anything, but I can talk to you about sex and orgasm. I couldn't talk
about that to Dr. K. I don't know why I can talk to you." I suggest to her that
she is feeling pushed away by me and wonder if it is about the breaks that we
have had and the ones that are coming up. She is disgusted with me, feeling
I'm very simplistic. "I am really disappointed with what you have to say. I
don't know why I don't go to see Dr. Z."

At some point in this session, I interpret her falling dreams as falling in
love with me and her fear of it. She rejects this at first, but then acknowl-
edges there might be something in it. I also suggest that she makes me unat-
tractive to prevent her from falling for me. She belittles this idea, but later
talks about wanting to relax and dance, perhaps falling into my arms. I suggest that there could be some sexuality in all of this, but she rejects it. How-

ever, she rejects it in a way that makes me suspect that it's true. She goes on to tell me about my narcissism, and how I need to be surrounded by women who adore me. Perhaps she feels hurt and jealous in the seminar, and perhaps I really don't need to be adored, and I could bear it if the class did not like me. She became quite relaxed during the session, as she was talking about how she felt about me, and went on to mention that she was going to get a face-lift and wished she could get a leg-lift, too, so she could wear short skirts. She feels that I am a leg man and that I like women's bodies.

Patient's Comment: It's so painfully clear to me now that my thinking Dr. Marcus preferred M derived from my perception of her as a genuinely good and gentle woman, whereas during this time I am feeling anything but! The intense need for the face-lift, too, is an expression of just how unable I am at this point to tolerate the experience of my ugly abuse of Dr. Marcus's love.

Analyst's Response: I recall that I believed at the time that the face-lift was some sort of acting out I needed to interpret, but I never found an opportunity to make that interpretation. It is all the more surprising since it is so easy to see in retrospect.

Patient's Comment: I believe your unconscious did the right thing. I can feel in my gut even now that I could not bear to hear from you on this matter at the time. I may have taken any interpretation you made to confirm that you, too, saw me as ugly.

The next day, Hope came in and talked for some time about a split. According to her, Dr. Z is wonderful. He has a mind. He's way up high, and I'm very low. She's ashamed of me. Other students in the class do not like me, they see me as Judas Iscariot, and yet, she has changed. She feels better about herself. She cannot understand why. The class wants her to present a case to me, but she is not comfortable and is hesitant. She went on to talk about being ashamed of her drunken father, but earlier on, she remembers adoring her father, who seemed to love her, but now she feels he just used her to make her mother jealous and get attention for himself. She feels I just use her, that I don't really care about her and I'm just interested in my own needs. She told a story of having to go down to jail when she was sixteen, where her father was in the drunk tank. She sees me as the drunken silly father. Nobody thinks much of me, and Dr. Z is the adored father. She can see the splitting. She felt betrayed by her father, who only cared for himself, and she sees me the same way. If she adores me, I'll betray her.

Late that night, she left me a message on my phone answering machine. She said, "I am feeling sad. I was feeling bad at the end of the day. I felt I had been bothering you. I tried to think that you would understand, and that lasted for a little while. Then I developed hypochondriacal symptoms and then psychosomatic symptoms and then a panic attack. I thought I'd call and let you know. . . ." I could not make out the rest of the message.

The next session occurred on a Monday. She said, "I felt I'd been hurting you Thursday. Then I felt anxious and had pain in my esophagus. I thought it was a heart attack. I tried to think that you were not angry with me but couldn't hold onto the thought. I became very panicky. Then I made the phone call and immediately felt better and went to sleep, but I'm sad, sad that I hurt you. I know there is a lot of criticism of you, yet I know you're a good analyst." I said, "Perhaps you were having an emotional heart attack. The pain of having to hurt the analyst you also love." She chuckled and said, "Like, perhaps, admire, even appreciate, but not love. There's a song in my mind. It's about a woman who sings that as a baby her fairy godmother picked her up and said, 'You will make your way with love, patience, and grace.'" (Later, she corrected grace to faith.) There was a lot about babies; what they were born with and what they get from their mother. Her mother often called her clumsy. It seemed to be important. Her mother felt that she, the mother, was beautiful and graceful, while Hope was ugly and clumsy.

I said, "You need me to be like a fairy godmother and see in you your love, patience, grace, and I think, beauty, that your mother could not see. Then you feel you will have access to those qualities." She protested a little while and said, "Babies are ruthless." I said, "Ruthlessness is a judgment term that we might give to a normal desire to survive." She said, "I feel very critical of you. I wish you'd make interpretations and not comments. I thought you were way off Thursday, when I was talking about my own violent behavior, head-banging, tantrums, breath-holding, taking off my clothes, peeing and shitting myself. I realize how sick I was. You thought there was something healthy about it, trying to tell my parents something. My siblings kept quiet." (I made some comment, which I could not recall after the session.) "I hate to complain, but that is sloppy." "You're trying to correct me so that I can be a better analyst for you." She said, "I'm very touched that you can accept my trying to help you. You really are a good analyst. It is in your person, so you should not be sloppy. I want to be proud of my daddy. If a mother handles her baby gracefully, the baby will become graceful. I'm very pleased with Brazelton and Winnicott. Now I see what you meant, that I was trying to tell my parents that there was something wrong."

After the session, I made a note that I had indeed been clumsy with her, clumsier, I think, than usual. Perhaps it is out of anxiety or perhaps intuitively so she could have the opportunity to correct me. She could not correct or help her parents to become better parents, which she desperately needed to do. Perhaps we are reenacting a piece of her childhood, but this time she is able to have a good effect on me which she was unable to have on her parents when she was a child.

~

Patient's Comment: I think Dr. Marcus's sense of clumsiness is in part derived from the accusations of clumsiness, which I also received from my mother. What is clumsiness in relation to love? Isn't it awkwardness, following the shame derived from many failed transactions—an inability to dance gracefully with love? But these painful attempts at loving with Dr. Marcus are not failing in spite of the cruelty mixed in.

~

I have no notes on the following session, only a comment that when the session ended, I had a feeling of slight anxiety, and I wondered if it was about the fact that she was going to present a case in my seminar later that day. At the seminar, the case she presented was beautiful. She was delightful and thoughtful. The patient would pun, such as on the word "foreplay," and then the analyst, Hope, would pun back. Later, the patient said, "Don't just stick it in," and the analyst, Hope, said, "Come as you are." There was a whole series of puns with sexual innuendo, which captured the essence of the session. My patient's unconscious was responding to her patient's unconscious in the patient's own language. I enjoyed the presentation very much, as did all the members of the class.

The next day, she began by telling me how, after the previous session, she had felt very good and it had lasted all day. Then, she went on to tell me she didn't like my apologizing in the hallway, that it felt wimpy. (There is no notation in my notes as to why I apologized to her.) "I did, however, like that you move fast for a big man. I think you could dance well or play basketball. My stomach feels full. I'm uncomfortable." Then she went on for some time about eating too much. I said, "It feels to me as though there is something in you that you need to express and are holding back." With some disdain, she replied that a feeling is not evidence, and she went on to talk at some length about how she rejects my statement. When she stopped, I said, "Even though my only evidence is a feeling, I still think there's something you need to express with some vigor, and perhaps you're afraid it might be too much for me." She said, "I'm smiling because you're like a Bobo doll. I hit you and you bounce right up. I like that you can make an interpretation based on your feelings. I feel I could vomit or have a bowel movement. From the books on your shelf, I think that Bion is your man. I don't know why I'm so pleased about how my presentation went in class. I can't believe they were really impressed with my work. It gives me a good feeling. I felt very confident after the class." After a pause, she went on to say, "I do have a feeling that I'm withholding something. I think it's that I like you, or love you. It reminds me of the patient in your paper. I find all the things wrong with you but I *like* you. I can't believe the other students really liked my work. It's frightening to like you; that's when you can get hurt, just as I got hurt as a child."

Analyst's Comment: I am impressed by how much I trusted my unconscious response, my feeling that Hope was withholding something she needed to express. Despite her rejecting it disdainfully, I was able to repeat it, this time adding that I thought she might be afraid that it might be too much for me. What I did not know at the time was that my capacity to persist with my unconscious truth relieved her anxiety about my weakness and enabled her to make contact with how much she liked me.

In the next session, Hope said she was feeling very good. She was getting good feedback about her work, and she was feeling very good about our work. She feels my presence gets into her and helps her regulate her autonomic nervous system, although she still has some trouble. Then her mood changed. She felt guilty because she feels she doesn't deserve to feel so good. Also, maybe it's too late for real growth and change. She started to have an anxiety attack. She recalled getting into a snit with her husband, but it was okay after they made love. A song came into her mind, called "The Interrupted Waltz." She would love to dance with me. I suggested that she is also excited and that this scares her. She remembers the colleague who had found her attractive and how uncomfortable she was with it. She wonders if it was okay for him to have those feelings. I suggested to her that we have interrupted our waltz, and she replied, no, she was still sitting on the sidelines watching. She hasn't dared waltz with me yet, although she called my attention to the fact that her body was leaning toward me. Then she pulled back.

Analyst's Comment: At the beginning of this session, Hope was letting me know that my work was good. I took it as a kind of supervision to continue taking risks from my unconscious.

Patient's Comment: Unconsciously, I think I might have been feeling that Dr. Marcus might find me attractive, and I was concerned about the ethicality of an analyst being attracted to his patient. Could I trust him? I certainly could not trust my father in this respect. Following the tantrum phase of my childhood, I became organized around the desire to be good, and to be perceived as good. My father seemed to position me in an idealistic island of safety in his mind, where I was not subject to his alcoholic lust.

~

Hope began her next session by stating that we were coming to our one-year anniversary the next month. She was very aware of the changes in her and knows it has something to do with me, but she can't put it into words. She doesn't know what it is. It's something about my presence. "Dr. Z says you should always be making interpretations, even if you don't say them. It's like a torrent of words. I learn from him, but. . . ." I say, "Perhaps it's the same with me. You know you get something but. . . ." "No," she responded, "It's a different 'but.' I couldn't be in analysis with him. What I get from you enables me to learn from him. You know, in biking, there are pushers and spinners. You seem to spin. I'm starting to spin. I always used to push. I worked too hard. You seem not to work so hard. i feel you just wait until something comes. You don't make constant interpretations. My body leans toward you. I want to roll my love to you."

I said, "I'm beginning to feel a warm, good feeling in my heart, even though I don't have words for it." She said, "That reminds me. I felt I was having a heart attack last week. Then I remembered your comment about its connection to love. Do you really feel it in your heart?" I said, "Yes, it feels like my heart, although perhaps it's my soul." "I wrote a poem about rolling grass. Gee, that sounds sexual. Rolling in the grass." "Perhaps," I said, "that's the only way you could express your love." She talked then a lot about what I had done that had helped her. "Perhaps," I say, "I was just here and it was my ability or capacity to feel your feelings that has been helpful." She replied that she felt hurt, and I asked her to say more. She said, "I just wanted to feel good about you. I didn't want your words." I said, "By trying to put it into words, I stopped doing what was helping you." At this point, she relaxed noticeably. "Of course, I can understand you'd like some credit." She talked about something between us that was palpable, but she wondered if it was real: "Something about your presence. Something about how you work. You don't make a lot of interpretations. I feel I can relax in your arms." At the end of the session, she had to ask for her bill, which I had forgotten to give her. Earlier in the session, she had talked about our only having three sessions per week, but she could see that it had some value. She could also see that my attitude of making the best of what we had was beneficial. She contrasted this with her own feeling of wanting to give her patients more than she could. She felt she was now becoming more like me.

～

Analyst's Comment: By telling of the warm, good feeling in my heart I was allowing my unconscious to tell her that I was receiving the love she was rolling my way and it made me feel good. While I did not think it consciously, my unconscious knew that this was a new experience that she needed. Her love was having a good effect, as opposed to the trouble it caused in her family.

Patient's Comment: Yes! In reading this now, I see how big a risk it is for me to put my love into expressive words, giving credit and appreciation versus criticism. I was clearly afraid of something, perhaps rejection, and tried to restrict Dr. Marcus's freedom to speak.

～

She began her next session by telling me that she knew that I was going to go to the training analyst retreat in Mexico. She felt I deserved it, that I worked hard. It is worth noting here that the reason I have notes on so many sessions around this time is that I was planning, if the opportunity should present itself, to use some of her material for discussion at this meeting. The material could be presented to analysts from foreign countries, who would have had no contact with either of us. She said that she had felt very tired yesterday and that it was a very difficult day, but her work went well because she trusted herself.

That evening, she watched TV, a program on ballroom dancing. She checked to see if I were right, if bodies touched in the fox-trot but not in the waltz. "I hated to see how I didn't trust you." I asked her if I was right. She said yes. "Also, at the same time, I read a lot about cancer of the breast. I'm beginning to relax a little and accept that I can't do all I would like for my patients." There is a particular patient who has no money, who needs more sessions, which she can't afford to give her. She was depressed by starting to see things more clearly, particularly the part she has played in damaging her objects. "What I did to you and my parents. I have a destructive patient, and I had to stop her. She was pleased that I stopped her, but it makes me sad." I said, "You do sound melancholy." She said, "It feels like a tornado hit my face." I said, "You couldn't help it that what you did seemed to be destructive." She said, "You mean my tantrums and head-banging?"

She went on to talk about something that caused me to interpret her "de-structiveness" as attempts to improve things, whereupon she began to cry. She said, "I'm sure that's true, and I felt guilty. I don't feel as guilty as I used to. I can accept myself better. I can forgive you for not giving me all I need, so I can forgive myself too. I've never said those words, 'I forgive you,' to anyone be-fore. I hope some day I'll be able to forgive my parents too. I don't know how you've helped me so much." I say, "It seems not to be through interpretation," and she said, "That's for sure. It's something about you." After a pause, she said, "What's that book on your shelf?" She said something which I didn't get, and then added, "Oh no, it's *Listening*. Strange. What a misreading." I said, "Per-haps you feel I listen to you." "It's not that. Dr. K listened. What I say seems to penetrate you." I said, "You mean it gets inside me." "Yes, and what you say seems to get inside me and affect me at a physical level." She said, "You've worked magic with me." "No, we've done it together," I responded. "Perhaps," I said, "without realizing it, we've been doing our own dance, as yet unnamed." After a pause, she said, "It seems as though we have."

Analyst's Comment: Hope is curious about how I am helping her since I have not been making elegant interpretations. What I did in this session was to present her with a different opinion about some of her behavior which had been labeled destructive when she was a child. I suggested that it was actu-ally creative. Recognizing the validity of this new opinion, she felt less guilt, which made it possible for her to contemplate forgiving herself, as well as the important people in her life.

Patient's Comment: I think there is some sense in which I expected that my loving expression of the previous day would damage or kill Dr. Marcus, and hence I was feeling melancholy. I am put in mind of the time my godfather visited and I ran to him eagerly. My mother remarked, "She's going to knock him over!"

In the next session, Hope came in and immediately began to talk about her very strong urge to reject me. She said she could hardly resist it. She wanted to attack me. It was a Monday session, and she said that all weekend she had been rejecting her husband. She had good reasons, but she knew she overdid it. She did not comment on it, but I noticed that she was on time and lying on the couch, leaning toward me. She went on, "I was passing gas and I shit in my pants, just the way I did when I was four, and I was about to add sarcastically that of course you wouldn't remember. That was when my mother had my brother Danny, who was heavenly to her. Then I was constipated, trying not to shit and spoil my objects. There's a song in my head which goes, 'Oh no, they can't take that away from me.' Who is 'they'? The spoiling me or you? It's about good things, like 'The way you kiss goodnight.' I'm jealous or envious about your wife's painting." I said, "I suppose it could be I who's going away, or you who's spoiling, or both of us, but there does seem to be a part of you who remembers the loved me."

She replied, "I see you on stage doing a soft-shoe. What is that?" I said, "No taps?" She went on, "You seem to know a lot about dancing. You take a knowing stance. Did you know that?" I said, "Not until you pointed it out." I felt she was somehow trying to correct me. She continued, "You look like Gene Kelly or Fred Astaire." I said, "That sounds like quite a good image." She said, "I feel weird dancing. When I shit in my pants at the age of four, no one understood. It makes me feel sad. My father called me Shitty Pants. My mother always said I had jealous thumbs. Maybe I wasn't just born jealous. Perhaps if I hadn't been humiliated and had been understood, it would have been okay. I feel you do listen, and we do dance some, but I feel rejecting of you again. I feel you don't want to deal with the shitty little girl me. You don't attend to her. You don't make interpretations about her. Dr. Z would make interpretations. You don't understand my anxiety."

I said, "You are anxious and my attention is being turned to other babies." She said, "Yes," and before she could go on, I said, "And perhaps you fear you won't be able to regain my attention when I come back from vacation." She said, "You make me work so hard. You don't really understand me. I don't feel held. I have to hold myself. You don't want anything to do with the shitty little girl. You only want the loving little girl who makes you feel good." I said, "You may be afraid I'm leaving because of your shitting." She said, "I still don't feel held." I said, "Perhaps that shitting little girl needs to know that she is loved too. That her attacking me is because she loves me and will miss me." "Yes," she said, "and that something good will come out of the attacking. I now feel your words are helping some." She seemed to relax at this point when I had to stop the session. As she was leaving, she smiled and said, "Have a good time." She is right about something, I noted after the session. I do have more trouble making interpretations with her than with most patients. I seem to behave like her parents. Then she corrects me, and I improve some. It does feel like an enactment.

⌣

Patient's Comment: It just struck me, too, that my repeated critical rejection of Dr. Marcus is an enactment in which, just as I was not able to think clearly about the rejection I was experiencing from my parents as a child, neither can he think clearly about what is happening between us while I am abusing him like this. But he does not react in kind. He suffers the guilt-anxiety (Winnicott 1982) and confusion that the repeated rejection produces.

CHAPTER SEVEN

~

Guilt

The reader may have noticed something that did not occur to me until writing a late draft of this book. Despite our different family backgrounds, both Hope and I suffered from and struggled with guilt. In Hope's case, she was convinced that she had really been a bad and shameful baby and child. She could point to her "bad" behavior, which she had to repeat in her analysis in order to allow me to help her understand it. My guilt was different in that I was not conscious of "bad" behavior. I was told of my "badness," but was not convinced consciously that I had been a "bad" child. In analysis, I could understand intellectually that I hurt my father's feelings by telling my mother that I would buy her a fur coat. I was committing in phantasy the "Oedipal" crime of killing my father so that I could have my mother, but it never felt emotionally true. Likewise, I could understand that I might have felt like a murderer because I tore my mother so badly when I was born that I prevented the birth of my siblings; but that, too, never felt emotionally true. Despite these good "Freudian" interpretations, I continued to feel guilty. Later in my Kleinian analysis, I was given the interpretation that I felt guilt for having enviously attacked my mother's breast. I found this interesting, but it did not ring true.

As an adult, I was shocked to learn, from a woman who had known my parents during the early years of their marriage, that my mother had had five abortions, which were illegal at the time. My scrupulously honest parents must have felt very guilty. Neither my analysts nor I could ever make a useful interpretation about this, but it occurs to me now, that in addition to any guilt of my own, I have been suffering my parent's guilt, which was too great for them to bear and was unconsciously projected into me. Although this had not been analyzed in me, my unconscious appears to have known enough to stop me from projecting guilt into Hope as her parents had done. Even when she invited me to do so, I refused. In recent work, Bail (2003) has put forward the idea that guilt is the very first lie unconsciously projected into the baby's mind, and it is this guilt that is so painful that we spend a lifetime trying to escape it. It gets passed down from generation to generation, from parent to child, until one person, perhaps with the help of analysis, is able to bear it long enough to recognize that it is a lie and not pass it on. Hope, I believe, was searching for someone to help her end this cycle of guilt.

While it would take us too far afield to discuss it at length, I would like to suggest that the Oedipus myth deals with this very subject. Laius and Jocasta, Oedipus's parents, projected their guilt into Oedipus, so that even though it is clear that his parents are the ones at fault, Oedipus accepts the blame. Part of our job as analysts is to help our patients know about the guilt that was projected into them as babies, and to be careful not to continue blaming the baby.

Patient's Comment: This is the best interpretation of all! In my tantrum behavior—banging my head, shitting my pants, even perhaps making a primitive attempt at suicide by holding my breath until I fainted—I was both accepting the blame and guilt for all that was wrong in our family, and also desperately trying to send it back to my parents for them to hold and think about. As I edit this book, now seven years beyond termination, I have just received a stunning gift of validation for this perspective from an eyewitness to my tantrum period—my brother who is three years older than I. We were talking about the heritage of shame in our family recently and he clearly recalled my "unpredictable" tantrums. It bothered him as he remembered how readily he joined in with the taunting. The next morning he said he'd thought it over and remembered "people talking about how all the trouble began when Hope was born." "I think you were made the scapegoat for the badness in the family," he said. What balm to my soul it was to hear this validation of what Dr. Marcus and I found through proceeding from our unconscious minds. And what a treasured moment with my brother!

CHAPTER EIGHT

Taking More Risks

The first session after the twelve-day break, Hope came in and said she couldn't stay very long because she had a flat tire. She sat up, but said that she couldn't look at me. "You haven't been interpreting my destructiveness. I make you goofy. You don't want to know about or deal with the destructive me." She then told a dream about a tall, thin man who looked like a former lover, who was very sensual but not thoughtful. "We were back in an old town. Then he went away. I was lonely and missed him. He missed me too. He also was lonely." Unfortunately, I have no notes about how this dream was analyzed, but it certainly does seem to be about the two of us and my going away, and also her feeling that we were lovers and that I missed her.

Patient's Comment: Again, I try to draw attention away from the work on loving to the destructive me. My unconscious, however, reminds me through the dream of the growing love attachment.

The next note I have comes from a session a week later, in which she mentioned that she was very resistant and then told me again of the song her mother used to sing, "Smoke Gets in Your Eyes." "First, [the singer] knows her lover is true, then she is rejected, and then humiliated." She said that she chooses to humiliate me first before I do it to her. The only note I have about her next session is that she had something that she called a heart attack in which she was really missing me, longing for me, as for something to put in her mouth. Then another note, five days later, in which she spent a short amount of time on her resistance and her constipation. Then she told a dream in which Dr. K was putting forward his wife for a position, and she objected strongly. She felt that she deserved the position. She associated to her jealousy, her Oedipal rivalry, which she never felt with Dr. K. Now, she feels safe to play with it here. This is our first anniversary, and she's excited that she will be able to go through her Oedipal struggle.

A song came to mind about a woman who has good sex with a man and then he drops her. She thinks it's about her hurt at the end of the session. She feels I am very present and that I just stop the session and send her away. In her anger, she holds back her feelings. She had dressed colorfully for this session and was hurt that I didn't notice and comment on it. She said she was glad my wife is a "colorist." She feels that I enjoy my colorful feelings. Perhaps I could also enjoy hers. She was pleased that she was starting to play. She wondered why I play with her. She was concerned that it was for my own needs, and she didn't like the idea of my taking care of my needs. On the other hand, she felt it was childish for her to just enjoy herself with me and not be concerned about me. She wishes she could do it, could just express her colorful feelings. She would like to adopt my wife and me as new parents. She felt we would take her to museums and shows, and she could bounce her colorful feelings off me, and I added, "They would be loved and valued."

In the next session for which I have notes, which occurred eight days later, she began by berating me for not paying attention to her destructiveness, not analyzing the destructiveness in her for getting a face-lift. Dr. Z would have done it. She told me I was only interested in her niceness. I didn't want her destructiveness. I didn't want to see it. I'm clumsy. My attempts at interpretation are slow and I'm not thinking. I found it difficult to come up with any interpretation that would shed light on her anxiety. It was clear she was anxious, but my attempts to get at it seemed feeble and were met with scorn and ridicule. I actually felt clumsy and awkward. I do remember that in the session, on one occasion, she felt one of my interpretations left her breathless with its beauty. I think in this session I was in the role of the little girl her, being made to feel clumsy and awkward by her mother, but perhaps I could have analyzed her attempt to cure herself with a face-lift. One thing that did come up, and perhaps it was the interpretation she found beautiful, was my calling attention to the smile she gave me when she had left the previous session, a smile rather than her usual frown. I suggested that I had given her a "face-lift."

Patient's Comment: Dr. Marcus is indeed giving me a face-lift! Although it may not seem obvious, I see myself showing increasing capacity for moderate, ambivalent expression in these recent sessions—loving and critical feelings are intermixed. I am not going away feeling terror about the destruction of Dr. Marcus's love and patience with me. I am calling him less frequently to apologize and reassure him. It remains curious to me why I provoked and "supervised" him so closely for so long. Perhaps I was searching for any trace of my intensely critical view of myself in him. I think one reason I wanted to hear more interpretations from the critical frontal cortex faculty rather than the unconscious was to enable me to examine his thinking more closely. Perhaps he was hiding bad thoughts about me? I eventually concluded that when he did not interpret, he was not hiding anything. In my provocative, scrutinizing behavior I remind myself of serial foster children I've worked with who seize control of who will reject whom by testing the limits to the maximum before they relax.

My notes for the next year are sketchy and very brief. Then, my notes for April 2, 1997, are as follows. Hope began the session by telling me that my greeting was neutral and she couldn't be sure if I were glad to see her. I told her that I was very glad to see her, but that I tend to be neutral and cautious with her because I find that I hurt her so much. After a pause, she said that she would prefer me just to be myself, and even as I was telling her why I was being cautious, I realized that it was unwise for me to be cautious. I told her that I agreed with her, that it would be better for me to just be myself. She went on to tell me about the dent in her nose and the possibility that it could not be fixed; she would always have a dent. It felt to her like a dent in her personality, something she never got and was still not getting, not getting the appreciation and acceptance that her work deserves.

Then she reported a dream. "I let a little girl patient of mine play with my regular jewelry, but I held the valuable, good jewelry back. I felt it was about my holding back with my patient, but I also feel it's about your holding back your best from me." The day after Hope had her dream, an adult patient of hers told her a dream she had in which she had let her jewelry slip into a pool. Hope took it up in terms of her patient's not valuing herself and her feelings but felt that her dream about the little girl had actually been about this patient. Hope felt it had something to do with her withholding her best from the patient—withholding herself. She felt she needed to give herself to her patient as I give myself to her, so Hope told her patient her dream and her sense of the remarkable conformity of the two dreams. It led to an extraordinary session, and she said that although she couldn't be sure of the outcome, she felt that they had turned a very important corner. I took this to be her way of telling me unconsciously how I could be of most use to her.

I thought about a dream that I had had the night before, when I was attempting to understand why I continued to hurt her so, and I said, "Perhaps you wonder if I care enough about you to dream about you." She agreed and said some things that made me suspect that she already "knew" about my dream and was telling me that it was important that I tell her about it. I made an interpretation along those lines, and her response caused me to think that it was worth taking the risk of telling her my dream. My dream had occurred after her previous session, in which I had repeatedly made comments that had hurt her. She asked me in that session if I understood why I kept hurting her, and I told her that I didn't know but that I was curious about it also. All I knew for sure was that I continued to hurt her. After an uncomfortable pause, she replied that she could accept that even though my response did not satisfy her need to know, she admired my capacity to allow it to remain unknown, without coming up with a quick explanation, like claiming that she was too sensitive. I pondered the question of why I hurt her so much, but nothing occurred to me that was satisfying. I assumed it was unconscious and that my best chance of understanding was to dream about the problem.

That night, I dreamed that I came upon one of my daughters and made a remark, which I knew, as I was making it, would be hurtful. I apologized to my daughter, saying I had no idea why I would say something so hurtful, and she accepted my apology. When I awoke, I knew that it was the dream I wanted, but the main question of why I hurt my patient seemed unanswered. My daughter is in fact sensitive and perceptive and very tuned in to feelings, her own and others. I used to hurt her a lot, and as a young adult, she was able to tell me about it; I was able to get it, and it brought about a major shift in my attitude and behavior toward her. We both changed and I became the father she longed for (whom I wished to be), and she became the daughter I always hoped for. What was significant is that despite all the difficulties, we both refused to give up on each other, and the result has been deeply rewarding for both of us. I knew this was part of what the dream was telling me.

On hearing the dream, my patient was pleased that I would want to ask my unconscious for supervision in her case. She asked questions about my daughter and was moved that I might think of her as a daughter. She apologized for asking so many questions and giving me the third degree. She told of a patient of hers who did the same thing, and she told him that she knew that he had to do it. "Just," I said, "as you have to do it with me." Again, she was moved and relieved. She talked about her thoughts of giving up her analysis, not coming fully to life, not expressing herself fully, and wondered if it would really matter to me. I replied that she was calling my attention to another reason for my choosing the particular daughter I had chosen to represent her. When my daughter was younger, she had had a life-threatening illness, and during the time that her life was in the balance, I became acutely aware of how devastated I would be if she died. As I told her this, I relived some of the experience, and my voice became very emotional. She commented on this and was moved deeply because she knew I was also talking about how much she meant to me. This was one of the most powerful, moving sessions I can ever recall in my practice. When she left, she turned to me and said, "Wow." I replied, "That says it all."

After this session, my strong belief was that by telling my patient about my dream and my associations to my daughter, I had enabled this patient (and myself) to have an extraordinary experience. Of course, she helped me be an analyst who was different from and better than I had ever been. That night, I had another dream in which my patient appeared as herself. We saw each other at a little distance in what might have been the lobby of a theater. She was uncertain about whether to approach me or walk away as though she had not seen me. Then she changed into another woman I know, whom I like, but who is older and less attractive. In thinking about the dream, I wondered if I was pulling back from the intimacy of the previous session. Was I afraid of my strong loving and sexual feelings? Was I concerned that she would retreat? Had I been too impulsive in telling my previous dream? Was there a way in which I could use this dream?

I was pleased to see her for her next session, which was two days after the previous session; I smiled broadly, but was aware of a concern that she would reject my smile and not return it. She did smile back, but began her session by telling me about her mixed feelings about the previous session. She felt I had been too impulsive in telling her my dream. Her patient was reacting badly to Hope having told her own dream. How could I be so sure that she was telling me it was okay to tell her my dream? While I was silent, I wondered if in fact I had been too impulsive. I had to consider that possibility seriously. She told me that she developed pain in her cranium and also noticed some irregularity of her cranium. She wondered if she was developing a brain tumor. I suggested that my impulsively telling her my dream might have had a damaging effect on her mind. She replied that the pain was like a pressure, and it made her think of the pain a baby might feel as it was being born. She remembers seeing her baby pictures; she had a large cranium and a little face. I added, "So, it may have been a difficult birth." She said, "The implication is that I was already difficult." I replied, "Rather than mother's pelvis being too small for your head." She said, "It reminds me of how I feel that your mind gives me a lot of space. I felt I was being born last session to a mother who was glad to see me. My mother was not glad to see me. It's so important for a newborn to see a mother's face that is glad to see her."

She made four slips in which she said that the previous session had been on Monday, rather than on Wednesday. The fourth time, she caught it herself. I called her attention to the other three and added that I hadn't called attention to them at the time because I didn't want to interrupt the flow. After a pause, she said that she got a little genital thrill, my word "flow" making her think of bodily fluids, and slipping and sliding and making connections. I cannot recall how we got there, but what seemed important was the correct stickiness, to make just the right kind of bond between us as mother and baby. She went back to my dream of the previous session, and asked some questions about my daughter and me. She imagined that my daughter had been difficult, and although she had been persistent in her attempts to get me to be the kind of father she needed, I must also have wanted to be the father she needed. I told her that it had been very important to me. (I did not tell her how grateful I was to have had an opportunity to repair the damage I had done to my daughter, and thinking about this after the session, I could see how we are repairing the damage done to her as a baby and child, first by her parents, and then by me in the early part of her analysis.) She had told me that I was helping her by being a "bad enough parent." I could now see more clearly how beautifully my dream had understood that the problem with my patient was similar to the one with my daughter, repairing the old trauma. One answer to my question of why I hurt my patient so much is that I had to hurt her to become the hurtful parent so she could then "cure" me by helping me become a "good enough" parent. She spent much of the rest of the session asking me questions and apologizing for having to do it.

At the end of the session, she asked for her bill. I didn't have one for her, and asked if I had not given it to her the previous session. When she said no, I said, "My bookkeeper must have failed to make it out." She replied, "Perhaps you didn't want to charge me." Then, as she left, she teased, "Perhaps I'll not have to pay." She smiled and looked at me in a way that felt very good to me, and caused me to feel hopeful that our experience together would have a very good outcome. Still, I worried, was I too impulsive? Have I done harm? The way the session ended made me think not, but only time would tell. Even if the results were good, would it have been better to be more traditional? Her previous traditional analysis had not given her what she needed, so I still think the risk I am taking is worth it. More of what did not help previously seems pointless. I later realized that I had her bill with the other bills and had overlooked it. Perhaps she was right about my not wishing to charge her.

~

Patient's Comment: I wonder if Dr. Marcus is not anxious about what he's let out with the dream—his deeply personal love for his daughter, and for his unpredictable patient. Along with his wish to make things right, he has made himself especially vulnerable to rejection. At least in part he would be identifying with my anxieties about loving.

~

At Hope's next session, which occurred after she had canceled her Friday session and after the intervening weekend, she came in saying she was all filled up, constipated. She missed seeing me. She was filled up with love. She felt that there has been a subtle but definite change in her. She is no longer anxious and irritable all the time. Little things that used to upset her do not. She now realizes that she used to be anxious all the time but didn't know that's what it was. Now that she's no longer anxious all the time, she is able to know about it. She said her patients are working on her to express her love. Between her patients and her analyst, she felt she was going to be able to do it. Telling her patient her dream had worked out very well. The patient came back with six more dreams and wrote her a very appreciative note.

Hope said she woke up with a song in her mind about cheat and cheating. There was also a song about "cheap." As we analyzed this, it led to thoughts about her father, who called her sisters cheap when they went out on dates with young men they loved. It was also about her father's jealousy of her mother's love for her children. She wonders, if she loves her patient, or me, is she cheating her husband? This was followed by a lot of material about her experiencing me as dead and dry and having flat breasts, which were not juicy. She longs for a good feeding experience but can't have it since her mother-analyst has flat, empty breasts. She felt very bad about saying such things about me, because she knows it's not true. I suggested it was an experience that she had had with her mother and needed to repeat with me, a mother who was not glad to see her, who was not full of joy and juicy breasts when approaching her. At the end of the session, I again forgot to give her the bill until she asked for it. We both laughed about this. It seems she may be right about my not wanting to give her the bill.

In the next session, there was quite a wonderful feeling, which we both noted. As close as she could come to describing it, she called it a healing energy that she felt she needed to heal the wounds in her soul. She needed the experience of being a loved and wanted baby. She felt that I really did want to baby her, and she wondered if I knew of the powerful feelings she would bring of love and hate and disappointment and poop. It was a very alive and exciting session, but she said the door between life and death is never far away. She hoped I appreciated the gift of her feelings. We seemed, she said, to be in a primordial mix where life could begin. She thought about what went wrong in her previous analysis, which had never reached this place. She added that because she had been so starved in childhood and was still so hungry, it was very important that I not try to feed her too much at once.

In the next session, she told me that the previous session had made her frightened and nauseated. There was a kind of nausea at her core. She had a mother who always felt she wanted too much, a mother who fed Hope an experience of herself that was nauseating and disgusting. She was pleased that I can see how when I give her too much, I make her sick. This nausea has always been with her at the center of her being. She is like a "failure to thrive" baby. She can't be fed too much too fast. Her life is in the balance. She feels she never came fully to life in her family. Her vigorous liveliness was not wanted. She needed me to know how precarious her situation is. She is on the verge of coming to life but might die emotionally.

Patient's Comment: I have the distinct impression reading this material now that I was also feeling like a baby who could not be fed this good food fast enough by her delicious mummy! Perhaps I was afraid of what my greed might do to him.

Analyst's Response: While the line of interpretation chosen may not have been the most accurate, the deepening of the material in the next session suggests it was "good enough."

In her next session, she said that after the previous session, she had felt very loving toward her mother and a song kept going through her mind, "You Were Meant for Me, I Was Meant for You." She felt that song also applied to the two of us, but she said she had become very anxious about an hour before today's session. She spilled coffee on herself, and she was afraid of getting germs from my door handle. She pulled back emotionally, but she felt that I also pulled back, that I was more cautious in the session. She thought that I was objecting to her wanting to move in like a little bunny, and she was afraid that I would see her as intrusive. She felt I hadn't responded to her song. I said to her, "You know, I almost sang it back to you." When she asked me what I meant, I then sang the first few lines, and then I said, "I think you're right. I did hold back." She smiled and the session went on about her fear of her love being rejected, and also her wish to have a rebirth with a mother who was pleased to have her, just the baby the mother had been waiting for. In some ways, it was quite a difficult session, but as she was leaving, she said, "Thanks for coming through," and at that moment, I felt very loving toward her.

She began the next session by talking about how lucky we both were to have found each other, and then went on to talk about a mentor who had deceived her. On the other hand, she felt safe with me because I seemed to be who I professed to be. She had read an article of mine in our society newsletter, which showed that I was the same with others as I was with her. She was pleased, even though she was jealous of my other loves. She said that she felt solid "here," pointing to her midsection. I noted the solidity that she seemed to give off and, as we talked about it, I suggested that it seemed to have a spiritual component. She was surprised, saying she had never heard me use the word "spiritual" before, but it seemed to her like just the right word. She went on, then, to talk about her religious feelings at some length. Again, she talked about how pleased she was with me that we were in fact like a mother and baby who were just right for each other. After the session, in my note, I state that there has been a definite shift between us in which I had a better feeling. My feeling is that whatever might go wrong, we will be able to repair it.

Patient's Comment: Dr. Marcus's telling me the dream of his daughter, and especially that he had requested the dream as a way of understanding better why he continued to hurt me, was a powerful turning point for me! He believed that he was indeed hurting me, rather than interpreting my experience as a transference distortion. It really got through to me that I was his analytic daughter, and mattered deeply to him. I registered that he would in fact be very disappointed if he could not become the analyst-father/mother I needed him to be. This changed everything. I began to feel we were a perfect fit— that sticky, bonded sensation. He needed me! He needed to make it work as much as I did. I agree we were home free now! We were going to be able to make it through the stalemate!

In regard to the forgotten bill and my comment, "Perhaps I shall not have to pay," I am reminded again of the poetic preoccupation I have had with the matter of cost as it pertains to relationship and to love. Love is a very costly commodity in human relationships, seldom flowing freely and reciprocally. In these marvelous sessions involving the gift of Dr. Marcus's dream to me, I experienced and took hold of the sense of our *mutual need* for a satisfying, loving outcome to our work. I began to feel less like a burden, less like a huge cost to him in my continuous demands. In fact, though I couldn't have articulated it at the time, I think it was here that I began to realize that he was receiving my demand for his authenticity as a gift of love! I was giving him something he needed in order to grow as an analyst. It began to feel like an even exchange.

Analyst's Response: In revealing my dream, I believed I was following my patient's lead, but I may also have been responding to my own desire to communicate at a deep level. What is particularly interesting to me is that at the time I told Hope my dream, I was not aware that I was telling Hope how much she meant to me. Because it came from my unconscious, Hope knew it was true. Hope's realization that I needed her reminds me that while we have no difficulty interpreting our patient's need for us, we may easily overlook how great is our need for them. As she notes, it was an even exchange in that we each got what we needed.

CHAPTER NINE

~

Risking Love

The following material is undated, so I don't know exactly when it occurred, but my guess is that it would be shortly before Hope decided to set a termination date. This is the way the note reads:

When she was feeling safe, she would often convey her feelings in the form of poetry, sometimes her own, sometimes the poetry of others. Often the poetry took the form of the lyrics of a popular song. One poignant lyric went 'Uncry my tears, unbreak my heart.' It was told in a way that made it clear that it went from the depths of her soul to mine. Tears came to my eyes and I experienced the heartbreak that she had experienced so many times when her love was rejected by both her parents. Of course, I interpreted how she now had to be very careful to put a thicket of brambles around her heart, to make sure it would not be broken again as it was broken by both her parents, and while my interpretation was important, it seemed even more important that I had actually had the experience with her of having a broken heart. She told me that she thought that even though I was empathizing with her deep sadness, that I was also reexperiencing some sadness of my own. I told her that I had no doubt that she was correct.

After a silence in which I began to worry that I had gone too far with my self-disclosure, she said, "I love you. I feel so fortunate to have found you." I was touched to my core and began to tear with love for her. I said, "I love you too, and I feel very fortunate to have found you." After another short silence, she said, "You seem to know exactly what to say to me, because you respond from your unconscious and your heart. I know that you are taking a risk in working in a way that many of your colleagues would look on with disapproval. I'm so glad that you are courageous." I wondered about her reference to my courage. I try to be courageous but often fail. It seemed to me that it was she who was somehow en-couraging me, and I told her so. She responded that her husband tells her that she is courageous, and I took that as a confirmation. After a silence in which I began to be filled with vitality, she said, "I feel so pleased that I am able to give you something. I never felt that I had anything to give my parents." I said, "I think it might be important for you to know that just being with you at this moment leads to my feeling wonderfully alive." She responded that she was becoming aware that she could have that effect on others. On another occasion, I became aware of a very good feeling in my chest, perhaps around my heart. I tried as best I could to describe this feeling to her, because I thought it might be a nonverbal communication. She told me that her broken heart was feeling healed, that our work together had a healing effect on her heart. I replied that it also seemed to be having a good effect on my heart.

The following vignette occurred around this time and was reported in an unpublished paper (Marcus 2002), but the exact timing is uncertain because the original notes have been lost. For the most part I simply described my feeling responses, allowing Hope to use my responses to understand herself. While it may appear at first that I am shirking my job as therapist, this way of working had the beneficial effect of enabling Hope to feel good about her own capacity to find out about herself. I report two sessions. My notes of the first session record only that I felt as though I were a mother with a baby sucking at my breast. My breasts were so full of milk that I needed my patient/baby to suckle to relieve the tension. We both remarked on the awesome beauty of the session.

Patient's Comment: I am reminded of Meltzer's (1992) work in which he talks about how a person can, in phantasy, emotionally live in different regions of the body. For example, a person might live in his chest and eyes, associated with the nurturing love and empathy of the feeding relationship. Or a person can live in his bowels, associated with waste matter and the urge to evacuate. As I so recently had said to Dr. Marcus that I was constipated with love, we might well think that my love had been stored up as something to be got rid of. In contrast, here Dr. Marcus's love is properly stored in his breast milk, with the overpowering need to feed his baby.

Hope began the next session three days later by talking about her heart problems, premature ventricular contractions, possible auricular fibrillation,

and her need to have an echocardiogram after our session. For about ten minutes we talked about her anxiety and her many physical problems, her fear that
she wouldn't live long, and so on. She wondered if there was structural damage
to the heart and she was pleased that I was an M.D. who knew about such
things. She thought that if she had it to do over again, she would go to medical school, but she didn't want to get sidetracked because she felt it was important to continue the work we had begun in the previous session. She wondered if perhaps she had emotional heart trouble. In the silence that followed,
I tried to tune into a sensation in my heart that I could not label. I told her as
much as I could about the feeling in my heart. When she asked me to tell her
more about the feeling, I replied that if I had to put it into a word, I would call
it "love." She replied that she had been meaning to tell me about three songs
that had been going through her mind. The first was "I'd Be Lost without Your
Love." The second was "Kiss Me," and the third was another love song whose
name I couldn't remember after the session. I told her that her associations suggested that my heart was responding with love to her love. This was followed
by a long silence in which I began to feel uncomfortable as though I had said
something wrong. I broke the silence by telling her how I was feeling and she
said, "When this current episode of heart trouble started I was feeling very good
after our last session. I then began to feel guilty, thinking I had no right to be
feeling so good. I wondered if I deserved to have such a good analysis. I bring
you such a sick baby without vitality." I responded by telling her that I felt very
touched and that my heart felt full, whereupon she began to cry. "I don't know
why I'm crying, I feel well cared for, and I'm such a sick baby."

"But a baby who is loving and gives me a lot."

"I guess I don't love the baby me enough."

"Perhaps, that is what is so sad, a baby self you do not love enough even
though she is such a wonderful baby."

"But so sick. I just want to be here and lie on your chest and rest."

Feeling the way I do when my baby grandson lies on my chest, I say, "And
it feels wonderful."

"I feel so much better. I notice I've turned toward you like a baby turning
toward the mother to have her skin against yours. I wish I had known you
when we were younger."

"You want to touch me and feel my skin knowing me the way a baby gets
to know her mother."

"Yes, and hear your heart beat, know you inside and out."

"I feel as though I'm holding a baby and it is a heartwarming experience."

"Is there something that might be able to cure my heart?"

"Perhaps."

"I feel so much lighter than when I came in. I feel like a baby who has had a good experience with her mother. I feel as though I have had all I need for today." (It's about two minutes before the end of the session.)

Hope, noticing a copy of a Monet painting of his garden at Giverny, says, "It's such a bright vital painting to have where I can see it. This has been a special session."

"Well, it has helped you see your vitality and perhaps has had a good effect on your heart."

After about three years of analysis, for practical reasons, we had to diminish the weekly sessions to a frequency of twice weekly, but despite that, powerful feelings were experienced by both of us. She told of the growth in her personal and professional life and was very grateful for what she was getting. On the other hand, she continued to be hurt and angry with me, and called my attention to my unconscious, subtle attacks on her, forcing me to go further in my own self-analysis. While this was a painful process for me, I was very grateful to her for having pressured me to grow.

Patient's Comment: Several times in this chapter Dr. Marcus has graciously accepted my reminding him of his hurtful comments or subtle attacks on me. I was still needing him to be the bad-enough parent who was also good enough to take responsibility for his contribution to my ambivalence. At the same time, however, I see myself continuing to make subtle, or not so subtle attacks on him with my "reminders," blaming him for my anxieties in regard to the growing loving intimacy. As I read this, I have powerfully in mind the image of the ugly and dangerous tapeworm emerging through my mouth, which could at any moment be startled into retreat, choking me. I make sense of this emerging tapeworm in terms of Fairbairn's (1952) paper on the repression and return of the bad object. I had obviously identified with and internalized the abusive and neglectful aspects of my parents, and done my best to hide these identifications, even from myself, through a painfully conscientious striving for a sense of goodness. While I was most abusive and neglectful toward myself, these attitudes and behaviors spilled over into all of my relationships, even though not so directly expressed as with Dr. Marcus. With him my abusive criticality of others was now boldly out in the open. Could I trust his love for such an ugly me? Was he going to bite back?

Only one serious problem remained after four years of analysis. She had not been able to make contact with and have access to her passionate sexuality. I got glimpses of it and could feel it, but each time, as it seemed about to emerge, she would pull back from me and the analysis, saying that she had had twenty years of analysis and enough was enough.

We explored her resistance from many angles but we were blocked until she had the following dream, which she described: "You and I were naked in bed together. I became unbearably sexually excited, more than I had ever felt before. I told you that I could not stand it anymore and asked you what we were going to do about it. You jumped out of bed and said, 'Don't worry, I'll get you something to eat.'" She awoke feeling hurt and embarrassed.

As we explored the dream, two interpretations emerged. The first was about her fear that I would pull back from her sexual desires, leaving her hurt and embarrassed because I might interpret her desires on an infantile level, and this made her resistant. The second interpretation was that I had in fact already pulled back from her sexual desires because of my own fear and was interpreting at the wrong level. Once I recognized the validity of the second interpretation, I began to feel the intensity of my own sexual desires toward her, which I was able to acknowledge. She was then able to answer the question she asked in the dream. She and I would not act out our sexual desires, but she could take her powerful sexuality home to her husband where it was appreciated. In addition, she found herself able to use it in her work where it added a new dimension. What I wish to call attention to here is that it was not enough to analyze this woman's anxiety about her sexual passion. She had to know that I was feeling similar passion and that we could and would talk about it. As long as I was afraid to feel the full extent of my sexual feelings, no amount of analysis would relieve her anxiety.

Hope told me that her husband claimed that she was castrating him. After associating to this for some time, she asked me if I felt that she was castrating me. I replied that I thought that she was wondering how much truth there was in her husband's complaints about her and if I could help her understand what went on between them. She agreed and asked me again if I felt that she was castrating me. I began to have a physical reaction of mild sexual excitement. We spent some time exploring her question and what she hoped to learn. Eventually, I felt that she could learn more about herself from knowing my response to her than by sticking to what was in her psyche. I said, "Well, I often feel a feeling that I could label as impotence when I make what I believe is a good interpretation and you seem to have no reaction, but at this time, I am feeling my own sexual excitement." She responded by relaxing noticeably and wiping a tear from her eye. "It is very helpful to know about my effect on you. The reason I hold back my response to what you say is I'm afraid I will have sexual feelings and that would excite you. I always felt I had to protect myself from my father's interest in my sexuality. It was always there but could never be talked about. I was very relieved that you were comfortable enough to tell me about your sexual feelings."

～

Patient's Comment: It is significant that here at last I am very moved by and able to tolerate Dr. Marcus's admission that I did, indeed, give him a feeling of impotence through my many rejections of his interpretations. It appears I am finally ready to face and take some responsibility for my own hurtful, cutting ways, which make me anxious as we move toward exploration of my sexual inhibitions. I wonder, too: Was it impotence I felt in my tantrums—impotence to get through to my parents? I think so! And I know without a doubt that it was inability to tolerate knowledge of his impotence to handle life that led to my father's cruel and terrifying treatment of his wife and children, passing the sense of impotence on down the chain. In this session I finally received evidence of Dr. Marcus's capacity to hold and reflect upon this feeling of impotence I had been communicating to him for a long time through my contemptuous behavior. I believe this knowledge gave me courage to proceed into exploring my sexual inhibitions with him, although I was not aware of the shift at the time. For the record, I do not remember my husband ever saying that I was castrating him. I don't think he would have used this psychoanalytic jargon. I may have been rephrasing his complaints about my disrespect as expressed in everyday controlling behavior toward him.

Analyst's Comment: There is much debate currently about whether it is ever advisable for an analyst to divulge sexual feelings for a patient. It seems clear that it was useful, and perhaps essential, for this patient at this time in this analysis, but might well have been harmful earlier. As is so often true in our work, we cannot count on rules, but must decide what is best at every moment, based on all the facts we have at the time. Sometimes the most important fact is what our unconscious tells us.

CHAPTER TEN

~

The Termination Period

Hope was having a physical problem with bouts of auricular fibrillation brought on by exertion or stress, and she felt that the ninety-minute drive to my office in heavy traffic was harming her physically. She had brought up stopping her analysis many times, and each time careful analysis revealed that she was running away. At this point, however, four years and two months into our work, she talked about stopping in a way that made me think that the time was right and that we might be able to use the three months she decided on for the termination period to contact and explore her sexuality. I was not entirely happy about a three-month termination period, which seemed unduly short to me, but she was determined.

Despite the fact that most of these sessions would have to be via telephone, setting a termination date appeared to free both of us to work more effectively. She requested, and I was able to give her, a third weekly session. One of the first interpretations I made to her in this termination period was that we appeared to be enacting the "Sleeping Beauty" fairy tale. Her passionate, loving, sexual self had fallen under a spell, and I was the prince who had to cut my way through an overgrown thicket full of brambles. I had to reach her and awaken her with a kiss. She immediately knew that this was true. She had to make it difficult for me so that she could be sure I really loved her. Her parents had broken her heart so many times that she could not bear to have it happen again. Each time she got her hopes up, she got slapped down. In the analysis, she reversed things so that it was I who got my hopes up, only to be slapped down. As she explored her "Sleeping Beauty" story, she realized that she wanted me as the prince to awaken her by finding her sexually irresistible. As she described her fantasies it sounded to me as though she might be familiar with Anne Rice's (1999) erotic version of the story called "Beauty." I chose to take the risk of asking her if she were familiar with the story, since her fantasies seemed to coincide with what I could remember of it. When she told me that she did not know the story, I chose to tell her what I could recall. In the story, the prince, after slashing his way through the brambles, finds Beauty asleep on her bed. With one stroke of his sword, he cut off her clothes and beheld the most beautiful woman he had ever seen. He awakened her by making love to her, after which he carried her off to his kingdom, where she was "forced" to submit to every possible sexual experience and was taught about life. At the end of a certain number of years, she was sent back to her own kingdom, having grown very wise and sexually accomplished. She found her own prince and together they ruled the land very well.

Patient's Comment: I think Dr. Marcus may be referring to the only conscious sexual fantasy I can remember ever toying with. It involved a number of young men, sexual slaves, doing my bidding. It worried me. I think the only perverse element in that fantasy was the omnipotence I needed to wield over the young men and, of course, that passion was not grounded in a private, loving, and respectful relationship, but associated with usury. I was never one to dwell in conscious sexual fantasy during sex, though, nor did I have any desire to do so. Although inhibited in orgasm, I fully enjoyed and was aroused by being present to intimate, sensual contact with my husband. So it was with a shock that I perused the Anne Rice novel Dr. Marcus mentioned, given the intense sadomasochistic nature of the sex portrayed: an exhaustive array of degrading tortures leading to sexual bliss, as administered by numerous impersonal "instructors." How could such sex lead to wisdom? Certainly, it was fear of and disgust with the fantasy of sex of this sort that prompted the need to control my sexual response to begin with. I had to admit, though, that a few of the sexual tortures were arousing to me. Soon the book became boring, however, with its repetitious sadomasochistic pornography, and I put it down. It caused me some concern about the nature of Dr. Marcus's sexual fantasy, and my own. I think it was actually a significant boundary failure and bad judgment on Dr. Marcus's part to refer to Rice's book in relation to me and to what we were experiencing together. It gave me an ambiguous access to the possible nature of his personal sexual interests and values, and left me with the lasting impression that these might differ greatly from my own. As in other instances, however, this failure turned out to be very useful, even vital, and worked for the good in freeing me to explore and express cordoned-off areas of my own sexuality within the safety of a relationship devoted to awareness and to setting my love free.

Perhaps Dr. Marcus's intuition to bring the Rice novel into the picture was also influenced by the fact that I had begun to explore with him unconscious phantasy regarding my parents' sexual relations. Their violent fights most often took place in their bedroom. My father was "insanely jealous," as my mother put it, and beat her when he thought she'd been unfaithful. One particular incident stands out when we children were huddled on the stairs leading to their bedroom, terrified. Suddenly, my mother burst through the door, naked and bruised, crying out to us to call the police. They were both drunk.

There was much confusion in my mind about love, sex, and trauma. From when I began dating I was afraid of sexual involvement because I definitely did not want to become pregnant, but also because I did not want to be regarded as a slut by my father or boyfriends. I saw how degradingly my father treated my older sisters when they began dating, and of course my mother! Nonetheless, being starved for love I experimented during college and after my divorce, with no great satisfaction with either love or sex. I can remember writing a book review years before starting psychoanalysis with Dr. Marcus. In it I said something about how it would be better to remain celibate than to enact perverse sexual fantasies, if this were the sort of thing that aroused one. I somehow sensed at the time that a perverse form of sexual organization was at the bottom of my carefully controlled sexuality, but I was much too ashamed to explore it, and I did not have hope that it could be transformed. Clearly, Dr. Marcus was on the right trail.

Analyst's Response: I agree with Hope that my mentioning Ann Rice's pornographic book was a significant boundary violation, and I was aware of it at the time. The fact that it came to my mind in association to Hope's material at that time, plus my experience with the good effects of using what arose from my unconscious, gave me the courage to risk asking Hope if she were familiar with the book. In retrospect, I believe it was part of a carefully devised plan by my unconscious to get to an aspect of Hope's personality which was vigorously defended and which I had not been able to contact by the usual analytic methods. Again, my unconscious knew much more than I knew consciously and the results made the risk well worth taking.

∽

Hope could not come to the office for her appointment on Friday, June 4, because she had to see a cardiologist about a breakthrough of atrial fibrillation. The telephone consultation went very well. She again sang me a song about her emotional broken heart. This song went "unbreak my heart, uncry my tears." There was much sadness for both of us as I listened to this song. Toward the end of the session, she said that she wanted to arrange an extra session the next week, but then added that she knew it was too late because our session was over. I said, "I'll wait." She said, "But my calendar is downstairs." I said, "I'll wait." She replied, "But it's quite a distance." I said, "I'll wait." She got her calendar, came back, and arranged the session. She said, "Next week, I'll try to see you in person. I like it better." I agreed with her, but I noted that I thought it had been quite a good session in that we had touched emotionally (I was thinking of the sadness we had shared). She said, "Yes, it was good, especially when you said three times that you would wait." This completely surprised me. I had not even thought about that part of the session, but apparently I had unconsciously seized what Stern et al. (1998) would call a "now moment" to make deep emotional contact.

There are two sessions for which I have no notes, but then, on Friday, June 11, she came to the session in great distress, saying that she was very tired, that her work tired her out. She was taking beta-blockers and another drug, but still the auricular fibrillation breaks through. She has been told by her cardiologist not to exercise, which takes something very important from her life. She thinks the beta-blockers make her tired, but without them, "it could be dangerous for my heart," she said. It was a session with much pain and sadness, which I felt in my chest. It was also a sadness that made me cry. At one point, she looked at me and commented on my distress.

Later in the session, as I looked at her profile as she lay on the couch, I noticed that she seemed to have the kind of beauty one might see in an old painting, perhaps of the Madonna. (She is very attractive but had never seemed so strikingly beautiful.) When there was a long silence, I said, "I don't know if this will be of any use to you, but I am having an experience which might also tell us something about you. As I look at you, I find you to be exceptionally beautiful. In addition, I feel a great pain in my heart because I feel I am unable to help you. It makes me wonder if that was an experience that you had with your mother when you were little." There was silence. I worried that I had gone too far. Then she said, "That's a beautiful interpretation, and it's right. I was always trying to make my beautiful mother feel better, and I never could." She then sobbed for five to ten minutes, after which she said, "I feel lighter. I don't feel tired."

⌒

Analyst's Comment: Although I still have some anxiety here about whether I had gone too far, I did not struggle about whether to tell Hope of my experience. It is clear I'm becoming more comfortable about letting my unconscious speak.

~

Unfortunately, the following notes are not dated, but I imagine these sessions occurred in July 1999, the middle of our termination period. For reasons that I could not recall after the session, I suggested that even though she felt fortunate that her father had not molested her, as he had molested her mother and her sisters, she might also have felt left out. In the next session, which took place over the phone, she told me that she felt it was a very important observation. She went on to tell me that she had bought *Lolita* a couple of years ago, but had not felt ready to read it until after our last session. She was interested in the story of a young girl who seduces an older man. She thought that she would like to be in that role.

As a teenager, she remembers being fascinated by the story of Nina, who was a prisoner in a concentration camp. Most of the women tried to make themselves sexually attractive to the Nazi guards, who would give them a candy bar in exchange for sexual favors. Even though Nina made no obvious attempt to attract the guards' attention—eschewing the rouge and lip coloring the girls managed to squeeze out of food or clothing, and walking in an almost unnoticeable way around the yard—she seemed to exude a kind of sexuality they found irresistible, so that she was chosen often, received many candy bars, and survived.

She expressed a desire to be like Nina to drive me wild with desire. In her family, after the disaster of the preschool tantrum period, she had found the role of the good, studious daughter, while her sisters were "sluts" in her father's deviant vision. She went on to tell me that the thought of having sex with an older man had always disgusted her, which was why she had been unable to read *Lolita*. She now was thinking that she might enjoy it, especially with me. She thought she'd like to be my Lolita. I suggested it would be a way of having a different experience with her father.

We started playing this out, but she didn't want me to act out her father's role. *She insisted that she needed me to be authentic, so that she could have a real experience.* At first, she was provocative, and I felt angry, although I did not tell her so until she asked me if I was angry. She asked me what I'd like to do to her, and I told her that I'd like to slap her. She was delighted. She said she'd slap me back, and we imagined a physical battle between us, which we both enjoyed. After the fight, she said, "I've just taken off my top and exposed my breasts to you. What do you think?" I said, "They're lovely." She said, "Do you find them exciting?" I said, "Very." "Would you like to fondle them?" I said, "Very much," trying to respond as honestly as I could according to my bodily responses. I was certain that even if this session had been taking place in my office, I would not have taken any physical action, and I felt certain that she could proceed only because she knew that she could trust me not to molest her. That is, while I was enacting her father's role verbally, she knew that I was different from him.

She said, "This is exciting," and I agreed. She said, "Now I've taken off the rest of my clothes, and I'm exposing my maidenhair and my vaginal lips. How do you like it?" I said, "Very beautiful and very exciting." I was indeed feeling sexually excited. She said, "I'm feeling very excited, and I'm very wet and swollen. Wouldn't you like to put your big erection inside me?" Feeling excited, I replied, "Yes, I can hardly resist my desire to put my erection inside you." She asked again, "Do you really desire me?" and I said, "Oh yes." She said, "Well, you'll never have me. So there." I said, "You can't say no. I'll force you." She said, "Calm down. Let me stroke your penis." I said, "I am calm. Now I'll enter you." "No," she replied, "you just came before you could enter, and I'm looking at you with disgust."

At this point, she broke off the drama and began to talk about what she had learned about her unconscious relationship with her father, and how this interfered with her sexuality and her relationships with men. It was interesting for me too in that I finally understood something that had been going on between us for most of the analysis. We would reach a place where it appeared she was ready to have access to and explore her sexual feelings and desires. I would begin to feel excited and hopeful. Then, the next session, she would talk about needing to stop her analysis. Her reasons were always very good. Nevertheless, I always ended up feeling painfully frustrated and unable to interpret what appeared to be considerable aggression toward me. Now it was apparent to her.

Patient's Comment: So here was my sadomasochistic sexuality after all. I had forgotten the second half of this session, in which I enacted a cruel sexual taunting of Dr. Marcus. That says something about how shameful it was for me! I did not know where I was going with this fantasy. We were both proceeding ad lib in the drama. But I see now that another "exorcism" was taking place: that part of my mother and maternal grandmother, and perhaps a long line of historical matriarchs, who conveyed contempt for their "impotent" men—poor providers, deserters, violent alcoholics. Certainly, this played a part in the many fights my mother and father had, with her responding to his devaluative, paranoid accusations with contemptuous backfire, which fanned the flames. She gave his contempt right back to him, at least until she became worn out from all the beatings. Dr. Marcus had remained himself through a lot of contemptuous treatment from me, but here was the sadomasochistic erotic core of it all, which had caused me so much dread that I had strangled my sexuality and passion at an early age. A very compulsive, overconscientious personality development ensued, with the disregulated and addictive patterns such constriction of needs encourages.

It was through the purposeful, playful enactment of this drama, *proceeding from our unconscious minds*, that I became aware of and able to tolerate and explore the anxiety and shame at the bottom of my soul, the relational defilement of love and desire. Neither of us had been able to gain access to my passion by any other means, even though our sensory-emotional contact was very fluid. Dr. Marcus's spontaneous participation was both exciting and cleansing. I think I was able to gain access to this shameful unconscious fantasy by which my passion was held in bondage because I was not just telling him about it—he was participating in the mutual, spontaneous drama. I think I felt accompanied, as though I had a partner in crime so to speak, so that the badness was not all mine. In fact, Dr. Marcus demonstrated the capacity to play with this sadomasochistic material in kind of an *innocent* way, such that I did not sense any voyeurism or other devious element in his response. We had worked hard to gain this kind of safety with one another over the years. We actually *embodied* the fantasy with gusto! My passion indeed broke through and I was able to take ownership of the perverse desire to allure and excite, then shame and humiliate. And surprise, surprise, it didn't turn out the way I must have expected. I was delighted! We did not engage in mutual abuse. Dr. Marcus did not become impotently violent, but he did want to slap me! He responded to my contemptuous dismissal with a potent perseverance to have me.

Yet there was something about his persevering with his excitement that felt clean. He wasn't intending to debase me, so much as to have me and to allow me to have him. I guess the excitement of that scared me and I broke it off. I now see that it was my fear of being overpowered by the desire to let go and to surrender to love and desire. It had always felt lewd to let go and have an orgasm, even with my husband, who beheld so much goodness in me; lewd, like the disgust I felt toward the baby drunk at the mother's breast. It felt dangerous as well. In the wrong hands you could get killed at the moment of letting go, like Diane Keaton in *Searching for Mr. Goodbar*. In Winnicott's (1982) words, your "going-on-being" could be disastrously disrupted and the psychotic anxiety of "falling forever" realized. We must feel safely held by love at the peak of desire. I wonder how many times I was dropped or not met in my erotic passion as a baby, a child? Even the best mothers and fathers can be uneasy with their child's sexual arousal or passion.

It is interesting to me that in order to break through to my sexual passion I needed the spontaneous dramatization of unconscious phantasy with a trustworthy other. Perhaps it does have something to do with temperament, but I think also with shame. Where the heart of love and passion are surrounded by a thick wall of brambles, a protective shame, it seems to take something of a miracle to get through! I feel quite naked and very vulnerable revealing our enactment of what can only seem a quite vulgar sexual fantasy for the world to see. In addition to the sadomasochistic element, the publication itself of this private analytic sexual encounter gives it the lurid feel of pornography. Nonetheless, I count it worthwhile to suffer this exposure in the hope that it will demonstrate the kind of risks an analyst might sometimes be required to take to release her patient and herself from an entrenched stalemate. Other authors are exploring this ground as well (e.g., Wrye and Welles 1994).

I found that in boldly owning this shameful unconscious phantasy within the safety of our analytic relationship, I experienced something of an interpersonal cleansing of my sexual passion. Moreover, the embracing of my sexual passion in a good way later generalized to other areas of passionate, loving experience and endeavor. In my case it has led to the recovery of my passionate love for my mother, a deeply exquisite fulfillment of love and passion with my husband, and increasing freedom to take risks in my work and with family and close friends. The risks we take with patients are indeed serious, requiring discernment as well as daring, such as Dr. Marcus has been at pains to elaborate.

Analyst's Response: Hope is calling attention to the need for both parties to take risks if an analysis is to be successful in freeing the patient of the prison of her deepest fears. In order to do this work, Hope and I had to develop trust that we were safe with each other. After four years, we felt safe enough to engage in the sexual play, which was healing. It is important to note that we were both aware that we were playing and knew that I would not attempt to act out the fantasies physically. As Hope notes, while we took a risk in working as we did, there was the perhaps even greater risk that, had we not taken the risk we did, she would have ended her analysis still in her mental prison. The sexual taunting in this drama might seem cruel, but because I knew we were involved in a psychodrama and the cruelty was undisguised, it was much less painful than the previous undercover excitement and frustration. This time I was mostly excited about how much we had learned from this nontraditional approach. While I felt anxiety working directly from my unconscious, I had learned with Hope that I could trust my unconscious and could also trust that she would not abuse it.

In the next session, which was also over the phone, she began by worrying that we were doing something perverse and actually having phone sex. Perhaps I was mentally molesting her, just doing it for my own pleasure. I began to worry that there might be some truth in what she was saying, but she went on to reassure me that she was aware of great benefit coming from our work. Although she still felt some disgust toward the father-me, she was very interested in having sex with me, and also with her husband. Although she and her husband had been fighting a lot about sex, they had been having more and better sex. At some point in this session, she said that she felt I had pulled back from her and from my speculation that we might be entering an enchanted sexual garden together. I didn't think I had pulled back, but since she was convinced I had, I said that I would think about it.

Following this session, I began to feel anxious and guilty. I wondered if I were in fact trying to have phone sex with her. Was I causing trouble in her marriage? There was no evidence for this, but my anxiety continued. Finally, I realized that my anxiety was mostly due to guilt, much of it from my past. I remembered how I was made to feel guilty as a little boy when I expressed my desires toward my mother. Perhaps I was also feeling my patient's guilt and perhaps also her father's guilt. Perhaps she was right, that I had pulled back. I may have gone further than I could go comfortably and taken more risk than I was ready to assume. That last idea seemed right to me, and when she asked me about it, I told her that I had invited her into *my* garden of sexual fantasy, which made me feel uncomfortable. I had to pull back from that, I told her, but I was quite ready and willing to follow her into her garden of sexual fantasies. At first, she was hurt and angry. She said she felt she had been led on and betrayed. At the next session, however, she was very glad that I could pull back when I felt I had gone too far because this was something her father could not do. In fact, she began to think it was absolutely perfect, exactly what she needed, to have me behave like her father and then behave differently from him. She talked about how well the analysis was going, how setting a termination date had seemed to free us both.

Patient's Comment: I was more than hurt and angry when Dr. Marcus said he felt uncomfortable leading me into his garden of sexual delights. I felt a sickeningly familiar betrayal at the height of arousal—that plummeting sensation in the pit of my stomach. I bounced back soon enough with the realization that he was right. In fact, leading me into *his* sexual fantasies would have tainted and maybe even ruined this stage of our work!

∿

She came to the office for her next session, hesitated briefly before lying down, and began by saying that she was going to try to seduce me. I made a sound to let her know that I was delighted. She told me she had been thinking about having sex with me all morning and was already wet. I said, "That's exciting" (and it was). She told me that my response increased her excitement. She went on to tell me that on the previous night, her husband, out of the blue, had a big erection, which lasted a long time. I told her that I noticed she was wearing a blue blouse today. When she did not follow me, I suggested that she might have had something to do with their good lovemaking. She replied that her husband said she had seduced him. "I'm so pleased," she said, "you have given me just what I needed, and I know you did it by following your unconscious, even by stumbling and going too far, and then recovering." I told her that I felt deeply touched and that she had now given me a very special gift. She replied she knew that it was true and she was pleased.

There was more to the session than I was able to reconstruct after it. At one point, when I was feeling very loving toward her, she turned to me and said, "You have such a loving look on your face," and she looked back at me lovingly. At another point in the session, she said something that touched me so deeply I began to cry. She said that it was sad that we were limited in what we could do together, that we could never physically make love, and I agreed. "But," she went on, "I am having the experience that a little girl needs to have with her father, to flirt outrageously and to know that she is absolutely safe." Later in the session, when she was telling me how well she was feeling, I was thrilled, and I told her so. She said that she was responding with a thrill in her genitals and legs. She was open and responsive. With her help, I had been able to give her what she needed. My guilt and anxiety were gone.

I have an undated note toward the end of the analysis. She came in and began by saying, "It feels as though we are now friends. Not that I don't still need you. I hope to have contact with you for a long time." I said, "Perhaps like a grown daughter." In the silence that followed, I felt intense good feelings. I decided to break the silence to call attention to the good feelings, and tried my best to describe them, but eventually gave up. Finally, I said, "The word that seems to describe the feeling the best is vital." She agreed and added that in the vitality, there was sexual energy and a bit of sadness. Another silence followed and I began to see an image in which the background was a deep, intense, beautiful blue. It persisted, so I decided to tell her about it. She replied, "I have been seeing the same color, and I knew you were going to call the feelings vital before you said it. When I'm with you, I feel young. It's not quite right to say I've taken in your youthfulness, but I feel safe to feel the lust for life I might have felt when I was little." She talked about how close sexuality and spirituality are. I suggest perhaps the word "eros" might be useful. She talked about feeling safe to feel alive and sexual. She was no longer frightened the way she used to be. She was beginning to enjoy her erotic feelings, although she was still just a little bit frightened.

At this point, the intense feelings seemed to diminish, and I called attention to it. She said she felt she was still staying with me. I said, "Perhaps I pulled back," although I was not aware of it. She quoted a poem from e. e. cummings. The poem was about two lovers and their effect on each other. Immediately, I felt the vital feelings return. She wondered how we would feel if we made love. I noted that the build-up of good feelings was so intense that it was almost painful. She began to cry, and I also began to feel sad. She said, "Because we can't make love, the feelings continue to build." I said, "It sounds like what I've read about tantric sex." She said, "It's so hard to label the feelings." After a silence, I said, "What comes to my mind is love." She began to cry again. "I feel my heart is opening to try to contain all the good feelings. My heart has been closed since childhood. It feels very healing for my heart." I said, "It feels healing for my heart too." She said, "I don't think of you as needing to have your heart healed, but perhaps everyone has had damage to their heart." It was a very moving and indescribably beautiful session.

Patient's Comment: In this session, I was able to feel the similarity of our experience, and my soul was satisfied. For example, I was overcome with passionate, loving desire seeking expression and perhaps relief through sex, and so was Dr. Marcus! Yet both of us were clear that to act on these desires would make something sordid of something beautiful, and completely defeat the purpose of our work. Love and desire would again become defiled. Again, I felt beauty and vitality between us, and so did he, even seeing the same cerulean blue! And we both felt the deep, intense joy and beautiful sadness of our satisfying, successful work coming to a close. Truly, my vital capacity for love and desire had been awakened!

CHAPTER ELEVEN

~

Discussion

Since each patient is unique, if we as analysts make emotional contact with our patients, we are forced to have unique experiences with each patient. Processing our experience leads to our growth. Certain patients, like Hope, require us, if we are to help them, to undergo major transformative growth. If we are ready, as I believe was the case here, the analyst can gain perhaps as much as the patient. If the analyst cannot grow, the analysis will fail to some extent.

The growth required of the analyst corresponds to the growth required of the patient—relinquishing old, familiar ways of being and developing new, more truly responsive ways of relating. With Hope, what I had to relinquish was my relationship to much of what I had been taught about how to practice psychoanalysis; the one thing I did hold onto was Bion's advice to practice in a state of reverie "eschewing memory and desire." I also held onto my own version of Freud's idea that our job is to make the unconscious conscious. I think of it as making emotional contact with the patient's unconscious. Since it is only our unconscious that can do this, I believe that we *must* have an emotional experience of our own.

While most of this analysis was conducted in a manner that I believe would be considered orthodox, some of the interventions were highly unorthodox and even idiosyncratic. It appeared that these unorthodox interventions, which were felt to be very risky, were the ones that promoted the most growth.

After reading a first draft of this paper, Hope wrote:

> I forgot one of the most important aspects of the way you work, which is so hard to find in a psychoanalyst. It relates somewhat to you not thinking in terms of "enactments" (perhaps a conceptual defense against finding oneself in the midst of a live drama with no prescribed lines). Anyway, it's your freedom to enter into the living drama of the transference/countertransference, to be a real life partner ready to take chances and say and do things which surprise even you! I needed that so much! And I can't believe I'm the rare patient who does. We know that in poetry and art forms in general, and in play as Winnicott (1971) described it, that it is surprise which breaks into joy, especially the surprise of dramatic encounter. And it's transformative. I will never forget the day I was playing hard to get, and you said you'd like to slap me, and I believe I said I loved it! Did you realize in just that instant you broke through my great anxiety of sexual love leading to abuse as it had between my parents, so freeing of my passion! Your response was the best kind of surprise, a true paradox when the very violence I feared became safe but lusty, loving passion.

The answer to Hope's question contains a central idea of this book. Consciously, I had no idea what effect my telling Hope that I would like to slap her would have. I only knew that we were playing a game that was both playful and serious at the same time. The rules of the game, which Hope had made clear, included the necessity for me to be completely honest with her. Many previous experiences with her had taught me that even though this was scary, it was safe. Or perhaps it would be closer to the truth to say that our work together had given me the courage to take the risk, even though I was defying what I had been taught. Another way to think about it is that my unconscious knew exactly what she needed, and I chose to respond from my unconscious. I kept trying to find the true Hope (the pristine, healthy, vital, creative her) by responding to her unconscious from my unconscious. My best responses were those that were not falsified by analytic thinking.

Perhaps the best analysis is done by our unconscious, but it takes courage to give up doing it the way we were taught, with theories that constrict us at the same time that they make us feel safe. Hope helped me develop the courage to use my unconscious even when I could not see how it was pertinent. One of the most important things for me that came out of this analysis is that I learned my unconscious was to be trusted. I learned it was much more than a seething cauldron of id impulses but was in fact a sensitive organ in touch with the truth.

CHAPTER TWELVE

~

Curative Factors (Hope Speaks)

As a result of the psychoanalysis with Dr. Marcus I have come to believe that interpretive understanding is the natural result of good analytic work together, and not the goal or essence of the work. During the analysis proper several simple but powerful interpretations eventually emerged. Some were spoken, at least two left unsaid and discovered along with others during the writing of this book. I believe that it was important to my digestion of the analysis that these latter interpretations remained implicit until I was established enough in love to receive them. An example would be the revelation of my abusiveness toward Dr. Marcus. More will be said of this delayed process below.

While the interpretations eventually proved enormously useful in my cognitive integration of what had taken place, my experience with Dr. Marcus suggests that a primary focus on interpretation in analysis may not only be superfluous to the engine that is driving the process, but even harmful to the successful development of the work. In this chapter on curative factors, then, I wish to focus on those *vital agents of change* I believe facilitated the unconscious flow of our work. I call these factors "agents" because they seem more like verbs or adverbs to me than nouns—the "how" versus the "what" that pried me loose and moved me through the sixteen-year stalemate of my career as a psychoanalytic patient. Salient to me at this time are the following:

1. The Development of Faith
2. Mutual Expressivity

3. Unconscious Attunement & Unconscious Responsiveness
4. Mutual Failure & Reparation
5. Mutual Risk-Taking
6. Spontaneous Interpersonal Play

In keeping with the spirit of this book, I shall speak of these agents of change in narrative style in this chapter, often italicizing them in the text to draw attention to how they came into play. Some material from the analysis as recounted above by Dr. Marcus will necessarily be repeated but from the perspective of my experience in the flow of the work.

In the Analysis: Agents of Change at Work

I believe that the robust development of faith in one another and in the work we were doing formed the cornerstone of the healing I received in the analysis with Dr. Marcus. I say faith deliberately rather than trust because, although certainly related, *faith more clearly designates the willingness to journey into the unknown.* Bion (1984a) used the word faith in this way to describe the commitment an analyst needs to resting in the unknown as each new session begins, trusting in the emergence of the unconscious process, when so often the patient feels threatened by working in such an ambiguous way. By this definition faith requires the acceptance of not knowing and therefore includes doubt. It does not depend upon certainty in dogma or theory, but is simply rooted in the willingness to enter into the journey of relationship with the other, not knowing where it will lead. With a proven experience of faithfulness over the miles, especially in times of pain or traumatic failure, the couple becomes confident enough to take greater risks together. In its essence then, *faith is relational.*

The analysis with Dr. Marcus was successful because from the start he demonstrated faith in dwelling in present experience, waiting for the unknown unconscious process to emerge between us "beyond memory or desire" (Bion 1967). In this way he often became aware of and expressed sensory or emotional experience which was received at a "frequency" below conscious apprehension and which spoke directly to my unconscious need. *These responsive interactions increased my faith in both our method and in Dr. Marcus's uncanny ability to really "get" at the truth of my experience.* He allowed himself to sink into the murky depths with me as the untraveled transference and countertransference began to unfold.

By comparison, my faith wavered greatly. While I actually loved proceeding clue by experiential clue, not knowing where we were or where we were going, I would recurrently seize up and try to close the process. The surprising turns Dr. Marcus would take based on his experience were exciting, but I was scared of moving through the unknown and my fear showed itself in those endless, biting criticisms for not offering up the neat, "complete" interpretations other analysts seemed to give. At times I actually thought that Dr. Marcus was just not that smart! Things he said or failed to say often hurt me. I did not trust in his competence. I wanted conceptual knowing, or so it seemed. However, I knew somewhere that a tidy, know-it-all approach would only leave me more frustrated. The paradox here is that while I often seemed to lack the faith to willingly travel into the unknown with Dr. Marcus, I was doing just that in *freely expressing* my huge ambivalence toward him! I wouldn't have dared do that with someone who claimed the privilege of knowing what was going on. *I was developing the faith that Dr. Marcus could stay with me, and participate in the painful confusion of my ambivalence.*

Dr. Marcus was emotionally responsive to me in ways I could perceive, and these responses seemed to arise both consciously and unconsciously. *He expressed himself to me in a natural, spontaneous way.* While demanding interpretations, I was all the while benefiting deeply from this *expressivity.* Of great significance, for example, were the delighted little sounds and welcoming words with which he met my timid overtures of loving regard. *He was not afraid to show his loving response to my love.* This was new! It enabled me to start to believe in my love, which proved vital to my being able to take the risk of showing him my unlovely qualities. *To me the fact that he continued to receive my love and to express his own in the midst of the long tantrum which ensued was more important than anything else in getting us through the stalemate.* In this way repeated failures of empathy on both sides of the couch were continually being repaired. What joy!

It was only quite awhile after we'd finished the formal analysis and had begun to write about our work that I realized we'd been working our way through the inherited stalemate during that whole long first phase. Reading Dr. Marcus's notes I saw with a shock that I'd been abusing him as he moved toward me vulnerably with his experience, perhaps like the vulnerable child I once was who learned through unavailability, rebuff and, most painfully, ridicule to hide her true self. But he didn't go into hiding with his loving gesture nor with his faith in our work, not even when I thought that I might have to leave this analysis, too. *Dr. Marcus simply remained himself and was able to consider that while doing something right in the work he was also doing something wrong.* I learned only later that he searched himself with some anguish trying to understand what it was. This was what I needed: A parent-analyst who could not only "take" my abuse but also realize that I was trying to make him think about his own areas of failure with me. *In fact, I needed him to actually fail me!* Staying in the messy drama with me, Dr. Marcus was able to do just that. What grace! A *bad-enough* analyst!

Winnicott (1982) introduced the concept of the good-enough mother, emphasizing that the child does not need perfection, just someone good-enough who gets it right more than 50 percent of the time. I think perhaps those of us who feel intrinsically bad also require a bad-enough analyst, too, who gets it *wrong* a significant portion of the time, at least for awhile, and who is secure enough to explore her failures with the patient. After he had searched himself for a long time, Dr. Marcus gave me a deeply healing, to-tally unanticipated interpretation *from his unconscious,* arising out of the dream about his daughter: *In my tantrum I was desperately trying to make a bet-ter parent out of him.* What a gift! He had identified a vein of gold running through my felt-badness, that badness now being alive in our interpersonal relationship and not only in my mind.

I was not familiar with the work of The Process of Change Study Group when I wrote the first version of this chapter. Upon discussing with me the agents of change I had singled out, a reader referred me to their paper on the importance of "sloppiness" in therapeutic encounter with babies (Stern, et al. 2005). This sloppiness seems to involve some of the same factors I've men-tioned here, although in different language, including the willingness to get confused, lost, to fail—the willingness and, I might add faith to get messy while working to get it right, *rather than assigning blame (overtly or covertly) when things go wrong.* Interestingly, not very long before learning of this re-search I had written Dr. Marcus an e-mail thanking him for being willing to get "dirty" with me in our work. I was thinking of his willingness to share the burden of guilt for our *mutual failures. This willingness together with his capacity to remain vulnerable and expressive throughout reinforced my belief in Don's va-lidity, that is, that he was the same person inside as he appeared to be outside, some-thing I had sensed from the start.*

Perhaps the need for a bad-enough analyst and for a measure of sloppiness in the therapeutic encounter were to some extent what Winnicott (1982) had in mind when he said that sometimes the analyst must *hold the situation* for the patient. Certainly, this describes what Dr. Marcus did during the pro-longed enactment of the as yet unnamed and unresolved tantrum with its necessary *repeated failures and repairs on both sides.* For Dr. Marcus to have in-terpreted my abusive treatment of him as it was happening would surely have derailed me. The tapeworm of my bad self would have rushed headlong back inside, choking off my new expressive life in the process! In fact, I was prob-ably provoking Dr. Marcus to interpret my destructive behavior precisely in order to avoid the injury and nightmare it would have caused me if he surprised me with such an interpretation (Fairbairn, 1952). Similarly, if we had tried to "work through" the abusive aspect of this first phase of the analysis after the breakthrough of my love and passion, I think it would have seriously sidetracked and diminished the trajectory of freedom to love that I was on when I left. I knew only that Dr. Marcus regarded the attacks I had made on him in the positive light of a child trying to make a better parent of him, and that was enough at the time. I was not yet able to tolerate taking personal responsibility for the pain I had caused him. It had taken so long to find someone willing to take some responsibility for the failures of relationship I had carried perhaps since birth.

However, three years following termination when Dr. Marcus and I began to write proved perfect timing. I was ready to begin to digest the graphic picture of my continual contemptuous criticism of Dr. Marcus as painted in his account of the first phase of the analysis. I don't think Don was trying to confront me with this picture. He was simply relating the truth of his experience in the analysis. But I was now able to admit that I had not escaped an unconscious identification with the abusiveness of my parents, nor the ongoing cost of this unacknowledged identification in relationship with both myself and others. Although my capacity to sincerely give and receive love had rolled forward following treatment, I felt stymied at this time by a continuing pattern of neglecting good self-care, even care as basic as getting enough sleep. Through our writing, integration of personal responsibility for my unconscious abusive tendencies in the analysis was to clear the way for me to begin to work actively and joyfully toward character and behavior change in this area. I am becoming so much more aware of careless, inconsiderate attitudes and behavior toward self and others; and recipient to the treasure of reparative opportunities. I thank God that the light began to dawn just as my husband became ill, and that I had almost four years of loving reparation with him!

During this first long phase of the analysis, Dr. Marcus and I also came to have a resilient faith in one another's character and motives in the analysis. When the going got really risky, we were both betting on each other's commitment to the work. We could take risks precisely because we did not suspect one another of ulterior, if unconscious motives, for instance, litigation or an actual affair. We both wanted to get through the stalemate and beyond. *Unwittingly, in our reparative efforts we supported the growth of courage and freedom in one another.*

Because Dr. Marcus and I had become secure enough to hold both the good-enough and bad-enough situations simultaneously, our relationship now began to draw out of me all of the frightening unconscious phantasy of desire involving love, sex, and cruelty—a toxic mix. Going there was a huge risk for me and yet I had good reason now to believe that it would not be turned back on me. The love and excitement were becoming more salient in our drama as Dr. Marcus continued to share his delighted responses to my loving expression. I could see clearly that he wanted me—he wanted my love! Although mothers and fathers are encouraged to attune to and respond to their baby's love and desire, mental health professionals are still highly scrutinized regarding such disclosures both within the profession and in the legal community to say nothing of the reaction to disclosures of sexual desire between patient and analyst! The patient also necessarily scrutinizes the analyst in this regard, wary of any repetition of former injuries in this vital area. What I found in Dr. Marcus was an analyst who could thoughtfully take the risk of disclosing the whole range of emotional and sensual states he experienced with me as they pressed into his awareness with some insistence, seeming to require expression. He was able to do this while conveying a primary dedication to our work. Such disclosure was absolutely necessary for me to gain the courage to continue moving past the stalemate into the arena of love and desire. *Through such disclosures I was able to make the necessary comparison between Dr. Marcus's analyst-self and his true self, that comparison we humans continually seek to make in order to determine whether the inside matches the outside and, thereby, whether we can trust the other.* I then was able to experiment with getting excited, overcoming the powerful fear of being slapped down. In fact, I was developing courage to try on many long censured emotions and states. *And so we began to be able to play together, with all of its spontaneity and excitement.*

As Winnicott (1971, 1978, 1982) repeatedly stresses, play requires the capacity to forget oneself, that is, to dwell in the present unselfconsciously. Moreover, interpersonal play is inherently exciting in its spontaneity: You don't know what's going to happen; you're not in control. Traumatized children and adults do not play. Like Humpty-Dumpty, they may take a great fall and fragment should they take a wary eye off their circumstances. They must carefully monitor their own expressions of feeling and impulse as well. Play requires trust in the "caregiving surround" (Stolorow, 1987). Winnicott (1971) also says that much of psychoanalysis is devoted to bringing the patient—child or adult—to the threshold where she can play. *I believe that this threshold or transitional area is the place where risks from the unconscious can occur, risks that can create the fertile interpersonal moments in which something new can happen and genuine change can begin to take hold inside. In the work with Dr. Marcus it became clearer that both the patient and the analyst must reach this threshold for such moments to occur.*

Here at the transition through the stalemate even our *mutual* unconscious resistance to forward movement became a matter for play. I remained dissatisfied with my capacity to abandon myself to love and passion. Although the more specific focus of my dissatisfaction was this continuing sexual inhibition, I know now that the inability to more fully surrender to passionate desire for and need of the other was obstructing depth of intimacy in all of my relationships, including that with God. I did not know what I needed in this area and neither, it seemed, did Dr. Marcus in spite of his urging me forward. I had developed health problems and was exhausted by commuting 500 miles a week. I guess I shocked Dr. Marcus by setting a three-month termination period. *In retrospect I believe that this was a daring, playful move on my part and that my unconscious knew that he and I both needed a kickstart to take the necessary risks. In this instance it was the patient who knew what the analyst needed!*

To my amazement the looming termination propelled us into what Kohut (1993) has regarded as a brief, healthy Oedipal transference, often experienced during the termination phase of a successful analysis. Perhaps, though, Kohut did not imagine such a highly dramatic engagement of sexual arousal, nor that anxieties regarding the perversion of sexual arousal could be resolved simultaneously! I had the need for Dr. Marcus's aroused participation in the *spontaneous play* which would arise. I didn't understand why at the time, but I needed him to proceed on *faith* with me, saying the lines that came to us with full passion. *It was a dramatic risk for him but he trusted in my unconscious and also in his own to lead him.* As it turned out the three months proved a perfect fit for the final act of the analysis.

Once past this initial hurdle Dr. Marcus and I again were able to be fully present in the work, allowing *arousal* to develop. In the neurobiology of attachment, a state of arousal in the analyst has been associated with enhanced neuroplasticity in the patient (Siegel, 1999), an opportunity for a "something-happened" experience to occur (Stern et al. 1998). This new research suggests that in addition to empathic responsiveness to the patient, the analyst's reciprocal *expression* of internal states is necessary for the development of secure attachment to occur. Perhaps "secure attachment" is another way of talking about what I have been calling faith. Pairing this research on arousal with Winnicott's (1971) thoughts on play and excitement, one can see the importance of the analyst's capacity for arousal and expressiveness in exploration of the patient's difficulties with love and desire. My intuitive demand that we play with passion spontaneously only added to the elements of arousal and surprise, and so to the potential for something to happen!

Before surrendering to my sexual love for Dr. Marcus we had to run an obstacle course of sorts. First of all, I had to realize I'd felt disappointed as well as special due to my father's apparent lack of sexual interest in me. Dr. Marcus's succinct observation of this possibility just here opened my eyes to a fact that now seems obvious. I suspect he'd held this thought quite a long time, and I am thankful for his restraint. Next thing I knew we were in the middle of Williams' (1951) portrayal of Stella and Stanley's hot, ambivalent passion for one another. One particular session stands out in my mind as startling in its healing impact. Dr. Marcus had shared his perception that I was playing "hard to get." When I asked him what he felt he truthfully replied, "I feel like slapping you!" Indeed, as my father had actually done to my mother on many occasions in their bedroom! I think Dr. Marcus may also have said that he felt like having me then and there, on the floor! At least that's what I see in my visualized memory of the engagement. Momentarily nonplussed, the next moment I was surprised by joy, laughing!

Somehow that spontaneous piece of play broke something free inside of me. Later I realized how afraid I'd always been that intense sexual desire would lead to a violent and degrading sexual intercourse and relationship, as I had reason to imagine behind my parents' bedroom door. At the same time I longed to play the game and taunt my partner, perhaps as I had witnessed my parents taunting one another and as I had felt teased as a child. Now I was having my chance! In retrospect I can see that what I wanted with Dr. Marcus was to see that he could experience a seething desire for me without violence. It is perhaps difficult for the reader to believe that in the frank act of interpersonal play related above I was totally spontaneous. Not only did I not know where I was going with it, but I seriously doubt I could have gone to that shameful place had I known. In fact, I think I needed *not* to know! I learned so much: That it was safe to explore and play with all of these inhibited sexual anxieties and states—we wouldn't damage our good relationship, as I had believed with my first analyst; I wouldn't be accused of wanting to "ruin" my analyst, as had happened when I told Dr. K. that I wanted to seduce him; I wouldn't get beaten, molested, or devalued for being sexual, a genuine risk with my father; and I wouldn't be kept at a safe distance by interpretation! It's amazing to me in retrospect that I became so confident as to require Dr. Marcus to stay in the spontaneous mode with me, speaking our lines boldly as they came to us in the moment, without any time for internal rehearsal or modification. While I think most analysts today believe that the patient is in need of a new experience, including a new version of an old failure, I appeared to need an experience which required the analyst to stretch way beyond comfortable, known territory, following the unconscious flow into spontaneous interpersonal play. I can't believe I'm the great exception. As in moments when we are caught out of role by encounters with our patients outside the consulting room, I think the passion of such spontaneous play moments within the analysis give opportunity for patient and analyst to reveal their true selves, hopefully validation for their genuineness of person.

As I became more comfortable experiencing my sexual love for Dr. Marcus, we began to experiment with where this would take us. Where were the boundaries? In the old debate, where was the line between analysis and gratification? As I pushed him to go further I can remember him saying one day something like, "I think I'm doing pretty good for an anlayst who was trained a long time ago!" Nonetheless, he did indicate that he felt we could experience anything and everything together, so long as we were motivated toward reclaiming my vitality. One day, in the context of his experience of having to hack away at what he saw as the "tangled branches" surrounding my sexuality, he asked me if I'd read Ann Rice's (1999) work, *Beauty,* as an example of the variety of sexual experiences people could have. "No," I answered and of course went right out and bought it. It was exciting but also anxiety provoking given the sadomasochistic flavor of the sexuality portrayed. As mentioned above, I think this was a mistake on Don's part but, as it turned out, a vital and courageous one answering to my unconscious need, and from which he recovered.

Encouraged by what felt like an invitation I let Dr. Marcus know that I was ready to follow him into his garden of sexual delights which I imagined we would explore "analytically," for the sake of my sexual awakening. I was startled next session when he announced pointblank that he would not lead me into his sexual fantasy, saying I would have to lead the way into any further explorations—that we would have to follow my fantasies! I felt the intense humiliation and rage of a child whose father has allured her desire deceitfully, only to drop her in midair. It reminds me now of an incident when my drunken father sat me on his knee, bouncing me and giving me all of the change from his pocket while my mother, who I picture ironing in the background looked on. The next morning when I looked for the change in my drawer, it was gone! When I asked my mother what had happened to it she answered only, "Your father's a fool." My thought has always been that she retrieved it, deprived as she was of household money by his drinking. I don't know when I next saw my dad but I do remember that he seemed completely oblivious of me and of what had occurred between us. I felt crushed and deeply ashamed. I feel sadness for all of us now as I realize he'd actually just been taunting my mother, and in such a pitiful way.

By the next session with Dr. Marcus I was convinced he'd done exactly the right thing. I saw that in my pushing *I'd been making myself available for an analytic molestation—really a very daring risk on my part, showing just how great my faith had become in our ability to unconsciously maneuver together through this minefield!* After a bad slip—another necessary failure—he had recovered and firmly redrawn the boundary, just as a good father does for his little daughter in the passion of her early "love affair" with him. I was greatly relieved! I did not feel dropped but protected. And I had learned for sure in his stumble that Dr. Marcus *really* found me desirable, just what a little girl needs to know in some sense with her dad before she moves on to other boys. *I reflect now that he had taken an extremely serious risk in following an impulse from his unconscious to get all of this across to me* by mentioning *Beauty.* For a moment he became the degenerate dad with perverse impulse, the bad enough analyst. I knew he would like to have me sexually. But then he proved he was not that dad but my analyst, intent on the successful completion of our work. Both he and I knew that further sexual explorations belonged with my husband. We were able then to turn to the sadness and joy of ending such a dynamic, fruitful work together.

Dr. Marcus's greatest gift to me lay in his unconscious responsiveness to my unconscious need and this involved the expression of his true self, the revelation of his character and person, which I found trustworthy. For example, his deep sadness and tears for the heartsick baby me, together with his expressed joy in being able to hold me close to his heart were profoundly affecting. Later, in his freedom to be just the passionate and determined Prince Charming I needed to awaken my sexuality, Dr. Marcus was a truly extraordinarily attuned dance partner! I am left with a lapful of such colorful snapshots of our time together, meaningful moments in which he responded to my deepest fears, needs, and longings, and in which my vitality was revived. In the writing of this book together, these moments of meaning have been woven into a beautiful tapestry of understanding, forgiveness, and gratitude. Surely Dr. Marcus was able to be just the mother and father I needed.

Analyst's Response: Hope has captured the essence of my work better than I have ever been able to articulate it. What needs to be added is how much she contributed by being just the analysand I needed to dare to work in the unorthodox manner with which I was beginning to experiment. Despite her protests, Hope flourished and encouraged me to continue working in the way that was good for her, no matter how unorthodox it seemed.

From the very beginning of Hope's analysis, I had two advantages over her previous analysts. Firstly, I was reasonably certain she had heard all of the usual analytic interpretations, which made it easier for me to avoid repeating what she already knew. I could wait for something not heard before to emerge. Secondly, Hope was able to tell me what had gone wrong in her analysis with Dr. K, thus enabling me to avoid making the same mistakes.

I believe that what we have called "taking risks from the unconscious" is my therapeutic response to what Stern et al. (1998) call "now moments." Each time I took such risks it led to a "moment of meeting" where we were revealed to one another authentically, while at the same time maintaining the psychoanalytic frame. What is fascinating is that Hope told me this in our very first analytic session when she was explaining why her previous analysis in the end had failed. She was convinced that for successful analysis to occur, patient and analyst had to allow their true selves to make intimate contact. I agreed with her, and although I had no idea how I was going to bring about the conditions where our true selves could make intimate contact, our unconscious minds found a way.

At the time I felt I was taking risks by revealing my true self and disobeying what I had been taught in many years of psychoanalytic training. In retrospect, I suspect that I was also afraid of the turbulence that would be caused by the intimate emotional contact of our true selves. In fact, powerful feelings of love, hate, sadness, desire, and frustration arose, and what seemed to be curative for Hope was that we could experience our feelings without harm to either of us. On the contrary, it had a healing and enlivening effect. We did not act on our feelings, but instead used them to gain understanding and, most importantly, it led to a change in both of us regarding our understanding of the implicit interpersonal relations between us. A new, exciting template for interpersonal relations was replacing an old, dysfunctional one for Hope. It could be different from the way it was with her childhood family.

"Now moments" are different from transference/countertransference because each member of the dyad brings an aspect of his or her true self to the encounter. It is tempting for us as analysts to call the emotions that are aroused "transference" because this makes us feel safer and less likely to act out. Nevertheless, because both parties are being their true selves, it is not transference, but a new and unique experience.

Some analysts, perhaps Dr. K, believe that the risks taken in this analysis involve too much self-disclosure on the part of the analyst. They believe that it is better analysis if the analyst keeps his true self and feelings hidden, which leaves aside the question of whether it is ever possible to do analysis without revealing something of our true selves. I believe previous analysts failed with Hope because they hid their true selves behind an emotional wall, which caused Hope to bang her head against the wall as she did when she was a baby with her mother. Had they not been wedded to their belief that self-disclosure is always bad, they might have been able to get this analysis back on track by recognizing their part in the stalemate.

I am in agreement with Stern et al. (1998) and others that interpretation alone is not enough to be curative in analysis. Something more is required. Stern et al. (1998) call this taking advantage of a "now moment" to have a "moment of meeting." Hope called it allowing emotional contact between the true selves of the patient and analyst. I agree with both and add that for me it has a spiritual quality of indescribable beauty. The rewards make the risks well worth taking. More analysts are now taking risks, and I suggest that good analysis cannot be done without it.

CHAPTER THIRTEEN

～

Before-After (Hope Speaks)

We need the tonic of wildness—
to wade sometimes in marshes . . .
At the same time that we are earnest to explore
and learn all things
We require that all things be mysterious and
unexplorable . . .
We need to witness our own limits transgressed,
and some life pasturing freely
where we never wander.

—Henry David Thoreau

I have always loved exploring the wilds, the thrill of being outside in the elements and of adventuring into the unknown. I suppose this penchant may first have shown itself soon after the tantrum period when I played outside regularly with two neighborhood boys. We were mad about cowboys and Indians, undertook modest sexual explorations, and bravely ventured out of our known territory of a few city blocks. When my family moved to what we called "the country," I was eight, and thrilled to have access to dirt! We had woods in our backyard and I would work up my courage to go walking in them alone, all the while terrified of losing my way. They were so magical in all seasons! It was my first taste of what Emerson and Thoreau have called the transcendental in nature.

Well along into my wilderness explorations I met my second husband in the unsurpassed beauty of winter in the mountains. (I had taken up skiing to stay warm outdoors in winter so that I might see the sights, not the other way around!) Hiking, bicycling, skiing, and snowshoeing together into the wonder of it all—oh, what marvelous fun we had! I felt safe following my husband beyond the edges of protected civilized living. He felt safe with me transgressing the boundaries of the stoical form of relationship he had known as a boy. We could not have foreseen how these adventures would prepare us for the boldest journey of our passionate life together.

Although I could not have articulated it at the time I came to Dr. Marcus, I was seeking in analysis to travel to an unknown and wild experiential place where something relational had to happen. I mean "wild" both in the sense of previously uninhabited, and also in the sense of out of my conscious control. When a child's emotional experience has not been considered thoughtfully and responded to empathically by the caregiver, it remains as undigested events in the psyche rather than remembered experiences (Bion 1984b). It is in this sense that I think of the unconscious wilds as previously uninhabited or unlived in territory. Similarly, one of the goals of analysis is the broadening of the mental capacity to explore new experiences. In our work together Dr. Marcus eagerly made space for and actually helped me locate these lost places where my love and passion were held captive by the dual tyrannies of terror and shame. We both had to transgress our limits and take daring risks to find our way into these mysterious, unexplored areas of experience and to accomplish the liberation of my love. For all that, while we have been able to identify factors which made our work successful, in another sense how it all happened remains mysterious and wonder-full to me. Not only did I come un-stuck and free to live and love with passion, but in this result I received exactly the equipment I needed most for what lay ahead.

Before

I had benefited greatly from the previous years of psychoanalytic work when I came to Dr. Marcus. Most especially, I had finally made a wonderful choice in love, or had love found me at last? Perhaps it was both. My husband was romantic and kind, and also responsible and accomplished. He loved what felt like the real me, and I loved him in the same way. We loved being married. Progress in healing was also evident in my being able to reach to the tantrum period in analysis. My body and soul were now full of that early emotional turbulence. I knew that analysis was the proper setting in which to let the tantrum play out, but I had not yet found what felt like the right partner. Dr. Marcus seemed a good prospect to my unconscious.

I continued to suffer from an inability to adequately regulate myself emotionally without recourse to the yo-yoing of compulsive and restrictive behaviors. I often worked to the point of exhaustion, denying myself adequate rest and relaxation. I was painfully conscientious, afraid of doing something wrong. Although my husband was very emotionally responsive to my needs, I remained unable to find a satisfaction which would take away the oral cravings present since my earliest days. Until the latter half of my college days, the craving was for sweets. I would overeat and then apply restrictive controls. As I applied for graduate school and my first marriage became shaky, I became insomniac, a condition I had suffered from as a young child. I began to use wine to relax at night and soon found that, as with sweets, I could not regulate my intake. Although for a long time I refused to consider that I might share the family vulnerability to alcoholism, I began applying controls over my use such as living with roommates and in communities where drinking was uncommon. At the time I came to Dr. Marcus I had "achieved" a stable restriction of both sweets and alcohol for many years and did not consider them problems, even though I continued to follow stringent rules of use to maintain control. I think the long reprieve I enjoyed from these cravings was enhanced by the love and security I enjoyed with my husband.

The most serious difficulties in living that remained as I started work with Dr. Marcus were also the least apparent to me. It is clear to me in retrospect that I was still a highly self-absorbed individual who felt interpersonally vulnerable, constantly on guard against negative judgments and possible rejection. I carried a hostile edge into relationships, though I did not see it that way. When criticized, I bristled and feared abandonment. This primitive self-concern infringed on my capacity for empathy and thoughtfulness toward others. The lack of gentleness I showed myself spilled over into my treatment of those close to me, often without my recognition. It is painful to remember how I felt justified in criticizing and attempting to control my husband, especially during our early years. We did become able to joke about my presumptuous attitude a few years into marriage, which brought comic relief, but it was through the work with Dr. Marcus that the foundations were laid for real growth in my capacity to respect the sovereignty of others. Though I was seeking an analyst who would expose his true self to me, I clearly was far from facilitating such exposure or from exposing my own true self as well! The fear of transparency compromised my professional work too, especially insofar as it was difficult for me to truly trust myself and my patient in intimate encounter. But how could I become more myself with others, given the unconscious fear and hostility inside? And how could I become kinder to myself and to others? I just was not sure that I was truly lovable, that is, truly *loving*.

How then could I dare to freely express my love? I was caught in a maze with no apparent exit. Enter my Don Quixote and the beautiful tale of rescue that was to be my analysis with Don Marcus.

After

The love for others came first. About a year after finishing with Dr. Marcus I experienced a dramatic upwelling of love and forgiveness toward my mother, and I began to understand her story. I remember it clearly. I was leaving the gym in a downpour, and as I drove toward the exit my new CD began to play a beautiful aria sung in the passionate and sad soprano of my mother. My tears suddenly began pouring down with the rain. She was singing to me a song of sorrow and love, telling me in Italian of her part in the failure of love we had experienced together. Of course, I don't understand Italian, but I understood this gift from above which my softened heart was ready to receive. This was the beginning of my conviction that something truly dramatic had happened in the work with Dr. Marcus and that it was a story that deserved to be told. Since that time I have continued to come upon experiences which empathically reveal my mother to me such that I can now sing her my own song of love and even regret for my part in our failures. For example, as with Dr. Marcus, my early and severe judgment of my mother's inadequacies must have compromised her confidence and effectiveness in handling me. No wonder she asked my father to take over during the tantrums—she must have felt quite helpless.

While it was this opening of the floodgates of love for my mother which prompted me to think about writing something with Dr. Marcus, in retrospect it is clear to me that unconsciously I also was getting ready to work over and metabolize the whole journey of the analysis. From this work was to come a new capacity to see and own my identification with the pattern of self and other abuse so core in my parents and in their parents. This long-delayed admission of fault followed naturally after Dr. Marcus proved able to admit his own part in our failures during the analysis. It would prove pivotal to my taking responsibility for my difficulties in loving well.

The love my husband and I shared was deepening during those first years postanalysis, along with greater tolerance of differences. Our ability to be open about conflict improved. For someone who had criticized her husband freely, I had been very sensitive about any criticism from him. Being a gentle man he had restrained himself from speaking freely to me about his resentments. Now, however, he began drawing a line in the sand in relation to my critical and controlling ways. He may have sensed some receptivity on my part, but I think he was way past ready! As I had with Dr. Marcus, I was increasingly acknowledging and apologizing for my mistreatment of him. In effect, my husband declared independence from my attempt to restrict his freedom to be himself. This abuse so mirrored my Dickensian stranglehold on myself! I am deeply grateful that I had this opportunity to learn to better honor his boundaries and to welcome his true self-expression while he was still well.

Our sexual intimacy took on a whole new quality. The word that comes to mind is "exquisite." In my new openness to desire I was able to experience for the first time my husband's highly attuned sensitivity to me physically. Clearly this had something to do with the development of a new physical sensitivity on my part. I was not so defended against arousal anymore and consequently was able to experience a much-heightened arousal, with no hint of the sadism I had feared was inextricably linked with sexual passion. We were now vulnerable and attuned in our bodies as well as in our hearts during lovemaking. I am so very grateful that we were able to experience these precious moments together before sickness intervened and increasingly impinged upon and ultimately curtailed the sexual expression of our love. I'm so glad I at last felt the release to surrender more fully to my husband's sexual love and desire for me!

It was about a year and a half following termination that my love for and faith in God welled up again. Though I had come to God in a new relational way in my thirties, my passion dimmed again during the long years of my third analysis. I think this was probably inevitable and necessary as I approached the tantrum, with all of its rage and despair. The reliance on myself rather than God undoubtedly also reflected the illusion of omnipotence by which I had survived for so long. The renewal and deepening of a vital spiritual life and commitment was, I think, just as inevitable after the work with Dr. Marcus where I had learned faith and love in a new and vibrant, reciprocal way. I had found how deeply indeed I could depend on another. While I had known this before with my husband—I knew how true a man he was and how dependable his love for me, I couldn't live it fully. Now my faith and love had come together in a vital, expressive way and I knew intuitively that God had given me the steady love and faithfulness of both my husband and Dr. Marcus as a tangible expression of His own care for me. The groundwork had been laid for the emergence and development of a passionate relationship with my God. This relational openness also began to be evident in the growth of loving intimacy with family and friends. Things were now in place for the trauma which waited just around the corner, the unimaginable journey with my husband through another unknown and scary wilderness. It would prove the most painful, most strenuous yet breathtakingly beautiful ascent we had ever made.

And so, three years following termination, my own true love was diagnosed with a Stage IV, slow-growing but ineradicable cancer. It had metastasized and filled his liver. He lived three years eight months after diagnosis. We were both so grateful to have that long denouement of our story together. Although he suffered the trauma of two huge surgeries and innumerable debilitating, invasive procedures, one emergency after another, he never wavered in his desire to live as long as possible. He was something to behold! Rather than become captive of cancer mentally, he faced each day determined to enjoy whatever he could, even when his range of choices had become so very narrow. I remember one day when I returned from work he said, "I told myself today, 'It's your job to enjoy this baseball game,' and I did!" It deeply impressed me how such a vital, active man in the end even accepted being able to do nothing but lie in bed holding my hand. He would press my hand and say with a big smile, "I've got what I want!" To my amazement and delight I was able to stay with my husband not only in the physical care he needed but also mentally, emotionally, and spiritually during our journey.

From the day he was diagnosed, self-absorption took a backseat to my husband's needs. I remember driving him around during those first days getting tests, retrieving biopsy slides, and racing to appointments. I searched to find an oncologist experienced with this rare cancer. In a strange way we were somehow happy in the chase together. He clearly was enjoying being carried by me not only in a practical sense, but emotionally! From the start and quite spontaneously, I felt an intuitive, even fierce determination to stay with him every step of the way. I was with him at the medical appointments, alert to how he was experiencing the news from doctors. I followed strong intuitions when medical advice didn't quite seem to add up. Together we sought out alternative possibilities, which twice or three times resulted in saving him from near death! It was always "we" who were going to the hospital, having surgery, procedures, or emergencies. We laughed at how this ubiquitous "we" slid into our everyday discussions of treatment and life, but I think it reflected a deep state of affairs wherein the "two become one" of marriage was being realized. OK, OK, perhaps my need to feel in control played a teensy-weensy part here, too, but it proved an asset this time!

My capacity to be what my husband needed during his illness and dying truly amazed and humbled me. The unconscious responsiveness I had received from Dr. Marcus apparently had become a vital part of me. Early in our journey, after one of two brutal chemo treatments directly to his liver, my husband was having a dreadful night in the hospital. I was emptying a basin of his vomit when I was stunned by a sudden, incongruent experience of joy. I almost felt guilty. The realization came that I was doing exactly what I wanted to be doing! It surely would qualify as one of the "now moments" de-scribed by Stern et al. (1998). I was to find that I actually loved taking care of my husband and it was a great surprise to me, who thought she would not make a good mother. It was the joy of sacrificial love. Of course, I felt some anger, fear, and resentment along the way, but very little toward him. The biggest frustration was actually with the workload and my difficulty in letting things go so I could just hang out with my husband.

Sadness was always there in the background or foreground. We grew so close that I often could sense his sadness and other feelings as if carried in the atmosphere of our home. For the most part it greatly comforted him when I would tell him so and join him there. We experienced joy in the freedom with which we could talk about our experience. We had many great laughs! I remember one day we were getting ready to go to a conference on this rare cancer and I found myself feeling angry. As I joined him in the closet I said peevishly, "I do not feel like doing cancer today." Grinning mischievously he countered in his big voice, "Well, I do not feel like doing cancer today, ei-ther," pulling off his tie with a flourish! He had a hilarious dry wit and was the easiest person in the world to care for because he responded with such delight! One day as he watched me changing a dressing he remarked at my having such an expression of concentration and concern on my face, and said I was the best nurse of all because I loved him. I cannot help but be reminded of that especially tender phase in the analysis when Dr. Marcus experienced holding me on his chest like his sick baby. He experienced the weight of me there and was so moved and grateful for this intimacy that he wept. It touched me deeply to know that in my exhaustion he experienced the weight of my long heartsickness as a gift to be shared. During that period I believe I was letting down the heavy weight of carrying myself through my life certain that if I only tried hard enough I would find what I needed to get well. And indeed I had, but in the end it was not my doing but a free gift. Now I was prepared to accept the weight of my husband in his illness and dying as an-other deeply sad gift to be shared, with joy and gratitude.

We held hands tenderly for hours during his recovery periods in hospital. My husband remarked once that these were among the happiest, peaceful moments of his life. He said that our love had made his life worthwhile. Like me, he too, had discovered that he could really love! A deep experience of emotional and spiritual healing was taking place for my husband as well as for me during this last journey together. Perhaps my fierce determination from the start, to stay with him and to care for and protect him to the best of my ability, was an unconscious response to his fear of being left alone in his helplessness, a fear of abandonment. Indeed, his mother was unable to care for him in the first three months of his life because of a scoliosis discovered during his lengthy and traumatic birth. It was the first time of many that he was left in the care of others while his anxious mother who was often seriously ill was hospitalized or otherwise incapacitated. At the same time his father was emotionally distant, and this sensitive child learned to adapt to an environment which did not recognize emotional reality. Through our intimate journey facing into death together I was surprised that in spite of the cancer my husband seemed able to revel in the deep security he felt with me. Now, through reflection, I think I understand better what was taking place. It was truly inspiring to witness the kind of deep emotional healing that can occur when a person is dying while being accompanied intimately by love. Just as a baby requires a mother's intimate responsiveness and participation to make sense of his experience, so too perhaps the dying, if they are to find the courage to stay alive to their experience as they face into death. Through my reliability and tangible delight in caring for him my husband seemed to experience a deep healing of this underlying fear of being abandoned.

Later, as he began to slip into a dementia consequent to liver failure and narcotics, my husband reenacted another signal traumatic failure from his childhood. For several days he had been crying and crying. As I lay with him, holding him as best I could with all the equipment attached to him, I remembered his story about when his two favorite uncles died in quick succession when he was seven. He had wept and wept then, to the consternation of his parents and whole stoic clan. They felt something was wrong with him. As we lay there, I softly told him that I thought perhaps he was feeling something similar to what he felt as a young boy when his two favorite uncles died. After a long and pregnant pause in the tears during which I thought I might have blundered, he suddenly cried out, "We're gonna die!" I knew it was the scared seven-year-old discovering death by himself, and able to say at long last what was "wrong"! I believe a new peace came to my husband through these and other moments of meeting. And I cannot say how deeply satisfying it is to me to have been able to "catch" these experiences as they happened, as one of my friends put it, and to facilitate his emotional and spiritual rest. Clearly, as so many know who have traveled this road before us, our opportunities for healing and moments of meeting can continue up to the moment of death if we are accompanied.

A few days before he died, my husband met with the social worker from hospice, a strong and sensitive man. Butch told me afterward that when he remarked to my husband that we were expecting four days of rain ahead he responded, "I won't be here." After awhile he seemed to arise again out of his exhaustion and spontaneously announced, "Hope and I are one." I will always wonder where it was my husband went during those silent minutes! What a treasure it is for me to know that he did not feel alone inside as he died. On the morning before he died I hovered near his face, talking with him and stroking him, telling him how much I loved him, how proud I was of him. He was sinking deeper into coma. Suddenly he opened his eyes wide, searching mine intensely. I could tell he was having trouble seeing, his eyes going back and forth, looking-looking. Or maybe he was looking into my soul. Then, almost imperceptibly, he raised his chin for a kiss and when I kissed his lips he kissed me back, twice. Then he sank back in, exhausted. Only hours later he began breathing mechanically, from the brain stem. I realized with a shock that he had roused himself one last time to come kiss me goodbye!

As an analyst I would like to add to this account that I worried needlessly in the beginning about the effect of my husband's illness and death on my patients, and about the timing of my gradual cutting back to a full leave of absence. The love that flowed through me to both my husband and to my patients would prove adequate to the challenges ahead. My patients learned early on of his illness because of my considerable time away during the process of finding help and undertaking the early arduous treatments. I wondered whether to reveal to them that it was my husband who was ill and that he had a terminal cancer. But of course they all wanted and needed to know, and I believe they would have known anyway, unconsciously, that it was the dearest person in the world to me. One patient opted for a referral, clear that he did not want to continue under the circumstances, a wise choice for him I think. Another new patient disappeared almost overnight. Others were in their termination phase and chose to stay with the process.

Most of my patients settled in for the long haul after testing their continuing security with me for a month or two, and periodically thereafter. With careful selection, I even took on a very few new patients during the second year of my husband's illness when things were going well, frankly explaining my circumstances. Not unexpectedly, the most important variable for my patients was my personal stability and capacity to be truly present with them in their hours, to retain room for them in my mind. Sensing this, they seemed able to forget my circumstances and to go on with their work, weaving the theme of loss into their personal stories in the most creative and unexpected ways. There was evidence that they found new courage to face into their own losses.

Surely the greatest source of my stability and endurance during the journey were my now vital capacities for faith and love which had opened up in the analysis and now were expanding exponentially in response to my husband's need. And I felt free as well to seek out the guidance and support I needed as I traveled through this strange new landscape. I found an invaluable, again vital connection with a psychologist who had cancer herself and who worked with people in the field who either had cancer themselves or in their families. We journey together still! In addition, my husband and I were surrounded by the love and care of friends and family. I enjoyed the particularly intimate accompaniment of a special friend who shared the emotional and practical challenges I faced daily, and who was much more experienced in care giving than me. As she would say, "We're in the trenches together!" My husband and me were not traveling this road alone. Obviously, the use of relationship to meet my needs had taken hold!

The other worry I had—whether I would be able to loosen my grip on my career sufficiently as my husband's need for me increased—turned out to be unfounded, as I very naturally adjusted to meet the changing situation. I had been married to my work for so long, but now love was setting my priorities in the right order. I began to let attrition take its course in lessening my hours so that I had the much-needed flexibility as my husband's degree of disability increased. As a result, several emergencies took place on days when I didn't have to be at the office. And I was able to prepare and make provision for my patients when I had to be away for longer treatments like surgery. I did not perceive that any suffered a traumatic disruption of their work. Still, my personal sense of being torn increased with my husband's need and I felt the wear and tear of carrying too many people who depended on me intimately. I think it must have been like what a mother feels when her very ill child or baby needs her and no one else will do.

My patients knew that I would eventually have to take a full leave of absence, and also that it was not easy to predict when this time would come, given the nature of my husband's cancer. When the time did arise suddenly, three years and four months from diagnosis, I scrambled to get more help at home while I worked to prepare my patients once a week for about three weeks. All who were left chose to wait. A few I spoke with by phone for another month but finally was unable to continue. I recall that as I explained my need for a full leave at that time a patient said tenderly, "You have been so present with me through this whole journey, you *deserve* this break. I know you will come back!" Another two patients confessed powerful feelings of jealousy and the "shocking" wish that my husband would die quickly or "just get it over with." I did not find this so shocking, however, and they knew I wouldn't. It was deeply relieving for them to know they could tell me and was evidence of great trust in our bond. The whole process with my patients, including the reunions that followed, has been rich and satisfying to me and to them. Finding that I was indeed free to prioritize my husband's care without resentment or fear as he needed me more is pure joy! I actually found out that I have a love for homemaking and front-line care giving, which I was not aware of before—another lovely gift.

The freedom to express and receive love during this most intense period of my life has begun to yield the fruit of treating myself, too, with greater loving-kindness in the wake of my husband's death. During the last year and a half of his life my self-care necessarily took a backseat. Given the looming loss, my history of jerky self-regulation, and the stress of managing his care, it is not surprising that my craving for sweets returned. I seemed without my previous capacity for restrictive control. I continued to take in an average amount of daily calories, but sometimes half of them were empty. At the same time, after intensely busy days caring for him I began to stay up late at night, reading and nibbling—"my time"—and suffered the additional loss of adequate sleep.

Eventually, given that we had been unable to go out for dinner for a very long time, I began to miss having a good glass of wine. I rationalized that after so long I probably could control my intake at home. I was quite pleased with myself in this respect for a while, but there came that evening when I couldn't stop at half a glass, or even two glasses! So I yo-yoed again between having no alcohol in the house for a time and then impulsively buying another bottle of wine to see if I could control my intake this time. You guessed it. It was then I found myself stating firmly out loud, "I am going into recovery after [his] death!" It was like I was declaring independence from the shame and denial at last. And by grace I followed up on that promise to myself! I'm so thankful for that decision which just arose up out of my soul unbidden, without thought! I am sure that the strength to make the decision derived from the love that had come to fill my life, especially the full expression of my love toward my husband. Guilt was at last giving way as I began to find love inside instead of judgment, fear, and hostility. Also, I had been well and truly loved by my husband, as I told him so often, and I was finding his love inside me as well as my own. To have taken the low road in grief would have represented the cruelest repudiation of that love.

I have no doubt that my ability today to make good use of active methods of character growth is founded on the liberation of my love in the analysis with Dr. Marcus, the considerable deepening of my spiritual life which followed, and the powerful expansion of my capacity to both give and receive love occasioned by my husband's illness. A book title which caught my attention long ago comes to mind: *How Shall We Then Live?* (Schaeffer 1976). I have needed a lot of help in learning how to live, and it has been given to me. I am immensely grateful.

Grief

My greatest consolations in grief and what make it bearable are twofold: First, I was wonderfully loved by "the best husband," as I used to call him. Because I loved and respected him so much, I could really trust that I indeed must be worth loving. Second, I was granted opportunity and capacity to express my love to him fully—verbally, emotionally, spiritually, and in every possible practical way. The work with Dr. Marcus was invaluable in preparing me for this honor. I am also greatly helped and inspired by identification with others who grieve, near and far, in our world, which is drenched in grief. Finally, I have before me always the daily acceptance with which my husband met his fate, "facing into death while facing into life," as my friend the psychologist puts it.

I have set off to explore these new wilds of grief in my own way, accompanied by the intimacy of friends. I find myself doing what I know best and what I had learned with Dr. Marcus—staying with the flow of my experience, including the play between conscious and unconscious. I trust in my unconscious mind because I believe that the spirit of God can move through it to draw me to the truth of my experience, which is where I have to start from each day if I am to go on authentically into my life "without" (Hall 1998). Sometimes I am not sure whether it is an advantage or disadvantage to have received so much training in tolerating painful affect, or to be so drawn to the unknown, yet I have befriended my grief. When people ask me what it's like, I find myself saying things like, "It is definitely an animal in its own right," or "Grief is an organic process." It is a sovereign entity, which I had best not try to control. I have continued to keep a journal, as I did during the journey with my husband. I cherish the many-colored sadness, the missing and longing for my husband, the tear storms. Our love was/is worthy of grieving. Grief is "slow time," a time to finger one's experiences delicately, a time of "breathing in the sweet, dark song of autumn rain," as I wrote in a poem once long ago.

Very often the emotions are preceded by a physical sensation or visual representation, a song, a poem, a memory—as with Dr. Marcus in our work. Turning the corner into the New Year I found myself literally "dragging," and upon inquiring what the sensation signified received a visual image of me attempting to drag 2006 with me, chained to my ankle. I did not want to start off my first full year without my beloved! I am interested in foreign sensations such as an utter lack of motivation. I try them on for size. I have the occasional burst of rage, but nothing major. I have come to see that if we are gentle with grief, it will be gentle with us. I am not in any hurry to clean out my husband's things or "get going," as one widow advised me. In a strange way, I am enjoying my slow, heavy grief time with its rich tapestry of experience. I am not without joy and meaning. In fact, I would describe my whole journey through grief, as with my husband through his illness and dying, as one of meaning-making. I hope I shall retain this capacity to walk slowly with my experience and that of others, staying with the wonder of it all, one foot in eternity.

Over the holidays, which I expected would be brutal, I experienced the first surprising, if fleeting sensation that I would be able to go on happily again some day without my husband. I sense that my new path is already beginning, again organically, interwoven with that of "Waving Adieu, Adieu, Adieu" (Stevens 1972). I have arrived at the confluence of suffering and joy and I wouldn't change a thing.

CHAPTER FOURTEEN

~

Postscript and Postanalysis

While writing this manuscript, and especially while revising it, Hope and I exchanged many e-mails, some of which I will excerpt in this chapter. These excerpts will allow the reader to judge for herself or himself something of Hope's current state of mind. I believe they make clear that Hope has continued to grow and to have a beautiful moving experience taking care of her dying husband. In addition, in these e-mails we take up some questions suggested by other analysts.

I wrote:

> Please be clear. I will not do anything with this manuscript that is against your wishes. Nothing will be included without your approval. I will ask your permission anytime I wish to present it. I do not think we need to show it to any of the others referred to in the paper. They may figure it out, but I don't think anyone is treated badly. I will do my best to preserve your anonymity.
>
> What you have written is beautiful and moving; it touched me deeply. It occurs to me now that you could always touch me deeply, so you had no need to bang your head against me. Or did you say that in what you wrote? Or perhaps you did bang your head against me by your many complaints which I took seriously, enabling you to stop. Likewise, because I spoke from my unconscious truth, I was also able to touch you. Touching has a very healing effect on both parties.

Hope replied:

> Thank you so much for your welcoming reply! After I sent the ms. off to you I felt some foreboding. When I reflected on my state I could identify anxiety

about what I'd revealed of my former analysts' failings or fumbles. I was able to see that I truly meant them no harm, perhaps even good—that analysts everywhere could benefit from learning to be more comfortable being known by their patients. I also knew that tracing the story line of my adventures in psychoanalysis was the single best way to tell my part of our story, as my unconscious clearly knew.

Secondly, I was able to identify dread about how much more of myself I had revealed in the paper, even to you. However, it is the truth of my experience that will best reach others' hearts and minds. Thank you for once again welcoming, loving my truth!

I wrote:

I'm happy that you have worked through and have come to terms with speaking your truth. While it can be painful and cause you to get attacked by people you thought were your friends, it also leads to finding out that there are many people who admire the truth and are thrilled to hear it. In addition, it tends to empower others to speak their truth, which for me is one of the reasons for writing.

I have been reading Langs' (1996) book on adaptation in the emotion-processing mind and many of the ideas he presents make sense. For some time, I have believed that Darwinian, or at least neo-Darwinian, theory was important as a factor in psychoanalysis, and is one of the reasons I gave up the death-instinct theory. If in fact a death instinct were embedded in the genes, it would very soon be selected out because the people who had that gene would not survive as well as individuals who did not have it. According to Darwinian theory, survival is based on adaptation to the environment. Babies, if they are to survive, have to adapt to the environment, usually the mother. These learned adaptive patterns become hardwired in the brain, and in analysis we call it transference. In a good mother-baby couple, the mother also adapts some to the baby, and they find a comfortable way to interact that is good for both of them. I think that is what we did. It was something we had to work at until we got it right. The thing about it is that it cannot be done consciously, which meant that I had to trust and be guided by my unconscious and to get validation from your unconscious, which you often did with phone calls. I think it is crucial that no matter what your initial reaction, your unconscious always came through with the truth (which I am convinced it always knows).

More from Hope:

We have started spending a week/month in the mountains and just returned from our inaugural trip. I did phone sessions. Seemed to work out OK. I definitely feel it's the right thing to do. As a result, though, I have even less time to focus on the many projects piling up on my desk, our paper being the priority. I did thoroughly reread your paper on the way home, though, and was deeply moved. I target next week for the (minor) revisions and my response. Again, your paper evoked a powerful response from me with more movement toward truth and healing. Thank you!

Another e-mail from Hope:

I've read your new version and made a very few changes. I tried to disguise myself just a little better by deleting what I considered some unnecessary information about me. Hope it's OK. Also, the title came to me: Hope, Faith, Love. I don't know how catchy that is, but I thought it fit our process perfectly: I came to you with hope, we developed faith in each other and the process, and my loving heart and expression was set free.

More from Hope:

I awoke yesterday with a dream: I was in the audience at your paper presentation and feeling uneasy. Then a close friend came and sat with me. I felt calm and we were all waiting for you to begin. You seemed to be doing something behind the podium and the audience was beginning to get restless when suddenly lovely old Victrola music came drifting over us: "You must remember this, a kiss is still a kiss. . . ." I started crying, feeling my deep love and gratitude for you.

My response is missing.

Another e-mail from Hope:

I wondered why this particular song, "As Time Goes By"? One thought that came to me is that our whole analysis together felt like that song and seemed to be in another time and dimension, like a movie, or beautiful music on an old Victrola. Analysis at its best certainly does seem to take place in another dimension. And the song comes from the movie, Casablanca, after all, where two people who loved each other so passionately could not in the end be together because of their loyalty to a prior, higher commitment. Our prior, higher commitment was to our spouses and to a fruitful analysis!

More from Hope:

[In regard to your reader's charges that we did not mourn the ending of such a good work] I think we did mourn, and not only regarding not being able to consummate our love sexually. There was that session, one of several, where you held me like a damaged baby and mourned for my health. I remember us speaking about how we could have twenty good years together if we were not an analytic couple and were not married to others. Most of all, the fact that we really went for the gold in the analysis is the best evidence that our mourning was fruitful, enabling us to get the very most out of the relationship we had as analyst and analysand, not holding out for unrealizable dreams. Isn't that what the early and late Oedipal are all about?

Another from Hope:

The hematologist thinks my symptoms are consistent with an autoimmune disorder in which the immune system manufactures an antibody that attacks white blood cells. Could also be chronic leukemia—let's hope not. Good news is my white cells were back up to 4.2 in his office last Friday, from 2.5. It's hard to diagnose because the antibody can only be found when the blood cell count is down. It's the least of my problems right now. My husband's bilirubin shot up again to 6 this week and he is jaundiced. (Don't know if I told you he was in hospital over July 4 with an obstructed bowel and bilirubin up to 3. It went down after that to 1.1.) A scan did not indicate any mass blocking the bile ducts. We are seeing a liver specialist Monday. He is weak. I feel so sad for him. I love him soooo much! He is such a uniquely wonderful man, with strong integrity, deep compassion. Illness really brings out a person's character, and his is something to behold. He continues to love me so well through all of this. I'm really grateful for our work that freed me to love him well, too.

From Hope:

I've been wanting to write you in regard to the way our work is continuing here in the valleys. I've had some pretty dramatic revelations, coming out of intense emotional experiences, which bring further healing in relation to the core work we did. I feel I am in the river of the Spirit's healing love and power, for which our work was so pivotal, that my uglies are coming more to the surface of my awareness, are more tolerable to me, and are melting away. Someday perhaps I will write it out. Thank you, Don Quixote!

Hope writes:

I've been missing you so much! And concerned. Are you well? Your going-on-being remains so important to me. You have given me so much! I only realize how much more and more. How was I so blessed to find you? It was the Lord.

What a journey [my husband and I] are on! It seems wrong by the world's standard to admit it feels like an adventure to me, so sad as it is. But at the same time we have never been so alive! It is exciting! Each moment a precious, eternal thing. Like our sessions.

My husband is dying, and I constantly pray for the capacity to be with him, right here, present. It is difficult. I want to jump ahead to the eulogizing, or back to the wild hikes, bikes, and skiing. I remember in my senses your presence with me always, remaining true to the moment no matter how much scorn I heaped upon you for your lack of "sophisticated" interpretations.

Somehow my work goes on with the core of my patients who have had the courage to stay with me through this dying-living experience. It is quite amazing, the work they are able to do around my life situation. I love them so much! God has given me my own children during this time of ultimate loss.

Thank you, friend.

I write:

I just returned form the meeting of the American Psychoanalytic in Seattle and had a chance to mention our paper briefly to Judy Kantrowitz and Steve Goldberg. Judy's precirculated paper was the topic and Steve was the major discussant. I was the only other person there for most of the time. Her paper was on the effect on an analyst patient of reading about his or her case material in an article by his or her analyst. They thought our paper/book is an important contribution, but had a couple of interesting ideas.

First, they suggested that your wanting to do it together had a meaning in terms of doing another piece of analytic work which had not been done during the analysis and that we needed to address that.

Secondly, they felt that if we wanted our work to be taken seriously, we would have to address the potential downside, such as what effect it would have on any future analysis if you wished to come back for more analysis. Would this destroy the analyst/patient asymmetry? Also, are we engaging in some kind of acting out? These are the kinds of criticisms they feel we are likely to get. Their point was that it would be important to ward off some of the criticism by letting the reader know that we have thought about the potential downside.

What do you think?

How are things going with your husband? I hope you are well. I know you are making the most of your experience. It is good to see how you are continuing to grow.

Hope responds:

Yes, these do sound like important questions to look at. I'm quite ill at the moment (bad cold), but I will keep your e-mail. How do you want to discuss the questions—by phone, by e-mail?

I reply:

> I think the best way to start might be for me to formulate and address the questions and then e-mail them to you for your comments and see where that takes us.

Hope writes:

> Thank you for doing the work of formulating the questions for us to answer. I actually pondered the question of why I wanted to do a paper together with you about our work, and also what it would cost me in terms of potential further analytic work with you. I have remained very satisfied with my choice, and it would be good to put it on paper.

I reply:

> While you have not answered the question of whether working on this paper together was unconsciously meant as a way of continuing your analysis, it does seem clear that it is and has been therapeutic. I'll work on the questions soon.
>
> As part of my literature search I have found out that Joe Schachter has edited a book in which seven analysts have written about seven patients and the patients were asked to comment. I will order the book, which has just come out. I e-mailed Joe about our work together and he asked if he could see it. If it is OK with you, I would like to e-mail him the version I presented in Santa Barbara. He has published widely and could be of great help.

Hope writes:

> Yes, to sharing our work with Joe Schachter. And thanks for always asking.
>
> Since the question came up, I've thought about my conscious/unconscious intentions in wanting to create with you some testament to our work together. I can clearly say I had no conscious intention of wanting to do another piece of work at the time. I simply thought that the results were so spectacular that our story needed to be told, whatever others might get out of it. I still think that's true. In addition, my sense now is that my unconscious knew I was ready to process and digest more of our experience together. As you will recall, I pretty much had amnesia for the process that took place during the first three years or so. Particularly, I was not really aware of how much I'd put you through and that, indeed, I had been abusive to you for quite a long time. To see that I had that abusive capacity in me, like my mom and dad, indeed is a gift at this time. I have been able to welcome the new understanding and to put it to work. My gratitude and love overflows to you, my husband, my God. Thank you!

I reply:

What a beautiful e-mail! You never fail to warm my heart. It reminds me that while in this period of our writing together, you have referred a lot to your feelings about your God, I do not recall that it came up much in the analysis, except on one occasion when I used the word "spiritual" and you noted that it was unusual for me. Is my memory faulty? It occurs to me that you may have felt your religious feelings would not be welcome. Perhaps they were present and I did not note them.

I think in these e-mail exchanges we have been doing some of the work of exploring the pros and cons of writing together.

Thanks for the permission to send our work to Joe Schachter. I have ordered his book, *Transforming Lives: Analysts and Patients View the Power of Psychoanalytic Treatment*.

Hope responds:

No, I didn't talk about God during the analysis because I remained alienated from him until I became reconnected to my love and passion through our work. I clung to God as a child and enjoyed an extended reunion in my thirties, when my faith became a living experience. But it had fallen away again during my analysis with Dr. K. Now my relationship with God is full with love and passion.

I reply:

As usual, your e-mail touched me and gave me chills. It is exactly what I needed. I may have to think some about my own experience of spirituality that does not include God in the usual sense, but has more to do with the awesome beauty of our world. Love and passion are two of the most important experiences. I am delighted by how your connection to God has been restored by means of our good work that never dealt with God by name, but perhaps was always about God.

Hope writes:

I have to tell you something about the further growth work I have found at this time with a wonderful psychologist who has cancer herself. I started talking with her in relation to the emotional challenges my husband's cancer had brought, but we have flowed into a deep work that integrates psychoanalysis and spirituality. She calls it, "Facing into death, facing into life." I grew so much with you in the capacity to be alert to the unconscious continually bringing to light areas of experience which need focus and relationship. I'm so glad you're sharing more of yourself with the world! I'm enjoying simple plea-sures with my darling here. Nothing could be more important. In spite of all, our sexual desire has not been diminished by my husband's illness! Our desire for every intimacy is enhanced.

I respond:

This is all so important. Perhaps a good analysis is one that opens a person up to be able to use whatever of value comes along in life. Like a good upbring-ing. You got exactly what you needed from our work together (as did I), and your growth does and will continue. Life is filled with mystery and excitement and sex, if we are open to it.

Later, I write:

I hope this is not a bad time for you, and if it is, I will understand if you are not able to respond. I do wish to run a few things by you, things that came out of my correspondence with Joe Schachter. His book, *Transforming Lives*, is good, but as he says, "tame as compared to our work." He makes the point that our work was almost all done in the transference-countertransference, which is cor-rect, but he did not get any sense of the problems in living that brought you to analysis with me and how they were resolved. While I do think that was cov-ered, if he is a typical analyst reader, it might be necessary to spell it out for the reader. Of course, you came because your analysis was stalemated, and as we worked, it became clear that you wanted to gain more access to and comfort with your passionate feelings of love, lust, and anger, or as I put it, "the wild, passionate, loving, and sexual aspect of your personality." And this was accom-plished. I think you'll agree, but let me know if you have any other thoughts.

He raised the question of why the fact of your not having children did not come up in the analysis. I wondered about that too as we worked, but it seemed to me that I never found an occasion when I felt it was appropriate to call at-tention to it. As far as I can remember, it never came up. Did I miss it? What is your memory of this?

Lastly, he asked what our agreement was about postanalytic contact. It is not in my notes and my memory is that we expected that we would have contact at meetings, and you would contact me if you felt the need for more analytic work. What is your memory of this?

Respond if and when you have the time. I know the painful, yet beautiful experience you are having with your husband occupies most of your time.

Hope replies:

I cannot give this the attention it deserves, but if I don't reply now I don't know when I'll get to it. I think these are good questions your readers are asking.

In brief,

(1) I did not really know what I was looking for when I entered analysis with you, only that I had not found it in my previous experiences. I did want a better sexual communion with my husband, but I really don't remember sex being uppermost on my mind, nor passion. I was filled with anger at the stalemate we'd reached in my previous analysis, and fighting the feeling of being the one who made things go bad. I don't really think I recognized my problems in living at that time, such as working too hard, to the point of taxing my health; being critical and controlling toward my husband; not realizing our intimacy as a couple could deepen greatly, as it has since; not knowing how to be a good friend, or how to find a good friend. And an addictive, controlling relationship with food; and past, intermittent history of drinking too much, so that I had learned never to drink wine at home, and to allow myself only a glass when out to eat once or twice a week. No, we really did not focus at all on problems in living, nor did I want to at that time. Too much shame, and besides I knew something had to happen (I just typed "happy") realtionally first that had just not happened in the previous therapies. Interesting second typo, "realtionally"—something real had to happen which made me a happier person. And it did! Looking back, I think I needed a safe relationship in which to find/be the abusive child/parent in me, and to find myself loved in spite of it all, or maybe because of it all. When we finished I knew I felt loved and loved you, I felt like a good girl and not a bad girl, and sometimes a beautiful woman, inside and out. But the outpouring of love for my mother did not happen until just before I first contacted you again, perhaps a year later. That love and passion flowed over into a powerful growing in all areas of my life, in which the "problems in living" have been and are being addressed and put right through helpful relationships, starting with my husband, whose loving capacity to help me grow even in his illness is powerful. For me, the sexual passion at the end of our work was a necessary bonus in which I was able to discover that, indeed, in being sexual we would not be the abusive and self-destructive couple my parents were. This opened the door for the exquisite intimacies that have followed (the sexual intimacy with my husband only, of course).

(2) It was not until a couple of years after we finished that I was able to find and admit to myself and others, starting with my husband, that I did not want children because (a) I was afraid of being an abusive parent, (b) I did not want the heavy dependency of children, which is how I experienced my mother as a child, weighted down, tied by ball and chain to us—she could not escape my father! At last I could feel my desire for children, which of course had led to my specialty with children in my work so many years before, and perhaps being a therapist in general. Not wanting children had felt like so much of a deformity that I had defended powerfully against awareness of that state. So you were right that you could not find an appropriate occasion. . . .

(3) I don't think we had any agreement about postanalytic contact. You never had any rules and I love you for it. I do know that I really felt finished

with my work with you and reiterate that I contacted you because of the overwhelming love which began to flow out about a year following our finish. I felt there was something important about what we experienced that deserved to be named and communicated to others. As it is, our working over the analysis together allowed me to understand more deeply what was accomplished, especially regarding my abusiveness. I'm so grateful. [Later note: Finally, in retrospect I believe that writing of our experience together has provided me with a necessary opportunity for creative reparation to you.]

Thank you!

I wrote back, thanking Hope for her reply, and I can now add my heartfelt thanks for her "creative reparation." She responded:

You're so welcome. I thought what I wrote was poorly written, given it was dashed off in a state of exhaustion. So glad it was helpful.

I like the idea of making "Taking Risks" and "Both Sides of the Couch" the focus of the title. I feel I took many risks with you, too, even with being abusive, and it came from my unconscious for the most part. I could flow forward from my unconscious knowledge of the work to be done because of the attitude with which you met my risk-taking, challenging material. I don't feel you ever took a step back or sat in judgment, but were steadily open and curious, welcoming, even excited by the challenges. I think this should somehow be touched on in the title as well, that is, taking risks from the unconscious on both sides of the couch, and how central this is to healing. And though I don't know if it's possible to include in the title, the focus of the book should further highlight what qualities in both participants makes such risks possible.

Love you! Thanks for working so hard to get our material out!

CHAPTER FIFTEEN

Gratitude

After receiving the first draft of this book, Hope e-mailed me:

> This is going to have to wait. My husband's pain shot up to unbearable levels this week and he is in hospital and I am with him. I am so grateful to you for preparing me to walk this road with my beloved.

I e-mailed back:

> Of course the book will have to wait so you can be with your husband. I very much appreciate your gratitude and I value your sharing with me the painful yet beautiful experience you are having. My heart goes out to the two of you.

By being fully present with her beloved husband as he is dying, Hope is having one of life's most painful yet rewarding experiences. She feels very grateful to me because her analysis with me has prepared her for this experience. That is easy to understand. What may be more difficult to understand is how grateful to Hope I feel for having been given the opportunity to analyze her and for the help she gave me by pressuring me to grow so as to be able to do it.

While I have no doubt about how valuable the analysis was to Hope, I cannot be certain about which of us gained the most. It seems to me that whenever I do good work, it is always because my patient has helped me. Perhaps a good analysis is one in which each party feels grateful to the other.

Hope's husband's health deteriorated slowly. In a series of moving e-mails she kept me informed of his progress and the beautiful, loving experience they were able to have together despite his failing health. Then one day she e-mailed her friends and family:

My husband died this a.m., very peacefully. The nurse who came afterwards pointed out that he had nary a crease of worry or pain on his beautiful face. He died facing me in bed. We had propped him up on his side last night to facilitate freer breathing. He was in full coma by then, breathing almost mechanically, like the spirit had left him. Nonetheless, I got up at 5:30 a.m. to give him his "comfort meds" according to advice from hospice, and then I went back to sleep also facing him, holding his arm. When I opened my eyes at 8:30 a.m., he was no longer breathing. He looked so beautiful in death! His blue eyes looking at me in a faraway, not empty, glance. I turned him on his back and we got to spend an hour resting and "visiting" before the hospice personnel descended.

The days before when he was laboring so intensely with every breath, I lay with him talking about this being our last tandem ride up a very steep mountain pass. As usual he was doing most of the work, with me providing good moral support and just that extra burst of turbo in desperate moments. "Just a little farther, darling, and we'll summit to a great expanse of space and freedom, beautiful vistas beyond our imagining! These shackles of your illness will fall away, and you will be free, in great spaciousness, inner and outer!"

When the mortuary drivers had carried his shrouded body down the stairs, I suddenly tuned into the American Angels singing, "In the sweet bye 'n bye, we shall meet in that beautiful morn. In the sweet bye 'n bye, we shall meet in that beautiful dawn, bye 'n bye." It's a beautiful CD. It helped me quite a bit in accompanying him out the door of our beautiful home. God is quite a dramatic arranger.

We will fly back East for the funeral now. When I return, I will plan a memorial service at our church, to which you all will be invited. Thank you for your love and support through this long climb! He is home free now, but I have some serious grieving and rejoicing to do.

Love, Hope

Bibliography

Aron, Lewis. "Ethical Considerations in the Writing of Psychoanalytic Case Histories." *Psychoanalytic Dialogues* 10 (2000): 231–45.

Bail, Bernard W. *The Very First Lie.* Unpublished ms., 2003.

Barnes, Mary, and Joseph Berke. *Mary Barnes: Two Accounts of a Journey through Madness.* New York: Other Press, 2002.

Bion, Wilfred R. "Attacks on Linking." *International Journal of Psycho-Analysis* 40 (1959): parts 5–6.

———. "Notes on Memory and Desire." *Psychoanalytic Forum*, no. 2 (1967): 271–80.

———. *Attention and Interpretation.* London: H. Karnac Books, 1984a.

———. *Learning from Experience.* London: H. Karnac Books, 1984b.

———. "Emotional Turbulence." In *Clinical Seminars and Four Papers.* Abingdon: Fleetwood Press, 1987.

Cramer, Bertrand G. *The Scripts Parents Write and the Roles Babies Play.* Northvale, NJ: Jason Aronson, 1997.

Dorman, Daniel. *Dante's Cure: A Journey out of Madness.* New York: Other Press, 2003.

Eliot, T. S. "Little Gidding." In *The Four Quartets*, 49–59. New York: Harcourt, Brace & World, 1971.

Fairbairn, W. Ronald D. "The Repression and the Return of Bad Objects (With Special Reference to the 'War Neuroses')." In *Psychoanalytic Studies of the Personality*, 59–81. London: Tavistock Publications, 1952.

Freud, Sigmund. *The Unconscious.* S.E. 14: 166–204, London: Hogarth Press, 1915.

Gabbard, Glen O. "Commentary on Paper by Jody Mesler Davies." *Psychoanalytic Dialogues* 8 (1998): 781–89.

———. "Disguise or Consent." *International Journal of Psychoanalysis* 81 (2000): 1071–86.

Goldberg, Arnold. "Writing Case Histories." *International Journal of Psychoanalytic Psychotherapy* 78 (1997): 435–38.

Hall, Donald. *Without.* New York: Houghton Mifflin, 1998.

Kantrowitz, Judy. *Writing about Patients: Responsibilities, Risks, and Ramifications.* New York: Other Press, 2006.

Klein, Melanie. "Some Notes on Schizoid Mechanisms." *International Journal of Psychoanalysis* 27 (1946): 99–110.

Kohut, Heinz. *The Restoration of the Self.* Madison, WI: International Universities Press, 1993.

Langs, Robert. *The Evolution of the Emotion-Processing Mind.* London: H. Karnac (Books) Ltd., 1996.

Marcus, Donald M. "On Knowing What One Knows." *Psychoanalytic Quarterly* 66 (1997): 219–41.

———. "Self-Disclosure: The Wrong Issue." *Psychoanalytic Inquiry* 18, no. 4 (1998): 566–79.

———. *Sex, Love, and Psychoanalysis.* Unpublished ms., 2002.

Meltzer, Donald. The *Apprehension of Beauty: The Role of Aesthetic Conflict in Development, Art, and Violence.* Gloucester, England: Clunie Press, 1988.

———. *The Claustrum: An Investigation of Claustrophobic Phenomena.* Gloucester, England: Clunie Press, 1992.

Mitchell, Stephen A. *Hope and Dread in Psychoanalysis.* New York: Basic Books, 1993.

Rice, Anne, writing as A. N. Roquelaure. *The Sleeping Beauty Novels.* New York: Plume, 1999.

Schachter, Joseph, ed. *Transforming Lives: Analyst and Patient View the Power of Psychoanalytic Treatment.* New York: Jason Aronson, 2005.

Schaeffer, Francis. *How Shall We Then Live: The Rise and Fall of Western Thought and Culture.* New Jersey: Fleming H. Revell, 1976.

Siegel, Daniel J. *The Developing Mind: Toward a Neurobiology of Interpersonal Experience.* New York: Guilford Press, 1999.

Siegel, Daniel J., and Mary Hartzell. *Parenting from the Inside Out.* New York: Jeremy P. Tarcher/Putnam, 2003.

Stern, Daniel N. *The Interpersonal World of the Infant: A View from Psychoanalysis and Developmental Psychology.* New York: Basic Books, 1985.

Stern, Daniel N., Louis W. Sander, Jeremy M. Nahum, Alexandra M. Harrison, Karlen Lyons-Ruth, Alec C. Morgan, Nadia Bruschweiler-Stern, and Edward Z. Tronick. "Non-Interpretive Mechanisms in Psychoanalytic Therapy: The 'Something More' Than Interpretation." *International Journal of Psycho-Analysis* 79 (1998): 903– 21.

———. "The 'Something More' Than Interpretation Revisited: Sloppiness and Co-creativity in the Psychoanalytic Encounter." *Journal of the American Psychoanalytic Association* 53 (2005): 693–729.

Stevens, Wallace. "Waving Adieu, Adieu, Adieu." In *The Palm at the End of the Mind: Selected Poems,* 113. New York: Vintage Books, 1972.

Stoller, Robert J. "Patient's Responses to Their Own Case Reports." *Journal of the American Psychoanalytic Association* 36 (1998): 371–91.

Stolorow, Robert D., Bernard Brandschaft, and George E. Atwood. *Psychoanalytic Treatment: An Intersubjective Approach.* Hillsdale, NJ: Analytic Press, 1987.

Tolkien, J. R. R. *The Hobbit, or, There and Back Again.* Boston: Houghton Mifflin, 2001.

Tuckett, David. "Commentary." *Journal of the American Psychoanalytic Association* 48 (2000): 403–11.

White, E. B. *Charlotte's Web.* New York: Dell Publishing, 1952.

Williams, Tennessee. *A Streetcar Named Desire.* New York: New American Library Signet Book, 1951.

Winnicott, Donald W. *Playing and Reality.* New York: Penguin Books, 1971.

———. *Through Paediatrics to Psycho-Analysis.* London: Hogarth Press, 1978.

———. "The Theory of the Parent-Infant Relationship." In *The Maturational Processes and the Facilitating Environment,* 37–55. New York: International Universities Press, 1982.

Wrye, Harriett K., and Judith Welles. *The Narration of Desire: Erotic Transferences and Counter-Transferences.* Hillsdale, NJ: Analytic Press, 1994.

Yalom, Irvin D., and Ginny Elkin. *Every Day Gets a Little Closer: A Twice-Told Therapy.* New York: Basic Books, 1974.

Index

About the Author

Donald Marcus is a Training and Supervising Analyst at the Psychoanalytic Center of California and the New Center for Psychoanalysis. Dr. Marcus was trained in "classical American" psychoanalysis, and then later had a Kleinian analysis with Albert Mason, and supervision with Wilfred Bion.